To George
from
Arthur
with friendship & gratitude.

# PERSPECTIVES IN
# HEALTH PLANNING

UNIVERSITY OF LONDON
HEATH CLARK LECTURES *1967*
*delivered at*
The London School of Hygiene and Tropical Medicine

# Perspectives in Health Planning

*by*

ARTHUR ENGEL

M.D.

*Lately Director-General
of the National Board of Health
Sweden*

UNIVERSITY OF LONDON
THE ATHLONE PRESS
1968

*Published by*
THE ATHLONE PRESS
UNIVERSITY OF LONDON
*at 2 Gower Street, London* WC1
*Distributed by Constable & Co Ltd*
10 *Orange Street, London* WC2

*Canada*
*Oxford University Press*
*Toronto*

*U.S.A.*
*Oxford University Press Inc*
*New York*

© *University of London,* 1968

485 26320 3

*Printed in Great Britain by*
WESTERN PRINTING SERVICES LTD
BRISTOL

# PREFACE

THE INVITATION to deliver the Heath Clark Lectures for 1967 was extended to me by the Senate of the University of London shortly before my retirement as Director-General of the National Board of Health of Sweden. This was at a fortunate juncture not only because I could reserve the time necessary for the preparation of the lectures but especially because I felt an irresistible drive at this turning point of my life to look back on the events of 15 years (1952–1967) of civil service.

This period has to a great extent coincided with an evolution in the medical field that in speed and abundance has no equivalent in history. To apply scientific progress to practical medical activities in an adequate way and without delay has been I believe a difficult task for every health administration. This has made planning activities, especially on the national level, a more and more important task. For consideration as a suitable subject of the Heath Clark Lectures I therefore suggested health planning with emphasis on hospital planning. My main contributions to the development of the domestic health services and to international health work have actually been in this field. Certainly my clinical background has been of importance for this orientation.

I thought I should not give a retrospective report of planning for health in Sweden and its practical results during my time. Even if I had to touch upon such facts the main purpose of the lectures should be to present a review of different approaches by old and new ways and means towards a well documented health plan. Of course a lot of subjective experience, belief and expectation will always invade the blueprints of a health planner trying to proceed in a scientific manner.

I always felt it a great advantage to be responsible for the health services of a country neither too small nor too large to be administered preserving local contacts. Sweden with its 8 000 000 inhabitants and firm administrative structure offers great possibilities for rational planning in health and social welfare. The socio-economic and demographic pattern of the nation is fairly uniform making country-wide planning realistic. The responsibility for providing individual preventive measures and medical care is firmly placed at the county level on one self-governing health authority. It is therefore easy for the central administration to co-operate with this limited number (28) of authorities; to keep fully informed of their intentions; to supervise them tolerably well and to guide them flexibly through an overall plan. I therefore feel and hope that our attempts to plan for the health of the Swedish people during a time of intensive medical and social progress may offer even foreigners some aspects of general interest—they may be experiences of the past or perspectives for the future.

I am most anxious to stress the great importance of collecting good statistical information not only on the services and their function but also on the output of medical training programmes and on the current availability of medical man power and of course on the changing pattern of disease and disability. The necessity for statistical registration of health hazards of the environment is commented upon. My attitude to health statistics has motivated a special chapter on this subject.

Screening for asymptomatic disease is considered in this book mainly as a public health method, expected to give information on the health of a population and perhaps, indicating needs and demands for health measures not otherwise observed. The trial we have carried out can also be looked upon as an attempt to master the increasing demand for health services in an era of insufficient numbers of health workers.

The function, growth and transition of the Swedish regionalized hospital and health system are presented briefly. It is the least speculative chapter but I have been informed from many quarters that our methodology and experiences are favourably looked upon.

The compilation of these lectures has required a lot of secretarial work. The main part of this task has been most competently taken care of by my former personal secretary, Miss Gun Berglund. I am deeply indebted to her for her excellent work. My gratitude goes also to my successor as

Director-General, Professor Bror Rexed, for his generosity in offering me working facilities on the premises of the National Board of Health. The chief of its statistical bureau, Mr Åke Sjöström, and his staff have been most helpful in providing statistical information and clerical assistance. Mr Sjöström was kind enough to read through chapter 2 and put his knowledge and experience at my disposal.

I must not forget to express my thanks to the Dean of the School, Dr E. T. C. Spooner and to the chairman at the first lecture, Sir George Godber, Chief Medical Officer of the Ministry of Health, for valuable advice and confidence.

To the Åhlén-Foundation I am most grateful for financial support primarily to meet my secretarial expenses.

In conclusion I should like to offer my gratitude to the Senate and the Academic Council of the University of London and to the London School of Hygiene and Tropical Medicine for the honour of delivering the 1967 Heath Clark Lectures and for the opportunity of having them published in such a dignified form.

*Stockholm, January* 1968                                                A.E.

Director-General, Research Division led, personally, in offering me working facilities on the premises of the National Board of Health. I am for its scientifical library, Mr. Lars Stedman and his staff have been most helpful in providing statistical information and valuable assistance. My gratitude was (and remains) too profound though simpler words can in fact hardly convey adequate expression of experience.

I must not forget to express my thanks to the Dean of the School, Dr. E. T. C. Spooner and to the chairman of the first lecture, Sir George Godber, Chief Medical Officer of the Ministry of Health, for valuable advice and guidance.

To the Alden Committee I am most grateful for financial support primarily to defray my secretarial expenses.

In conclusion I should like to offer my thanks to the Senate and the Academic Council of the University of London and to the London School of Hygiene and Tropical Medicine, for the honour of delivering the 1967 Heath Clark Lectures and for the opportunity of bringing together a number of my original ideas.

Stockholm, January 1968.

# CONTENTS

1. HEALTH PLANNING IN A CHANGING SOCIETY   1
2. STATISTICS AND HEALTH PLANNING   26
3. MASS SCREENING FOR ASYMPTOMATIC DISEASE AS A PUBLIC HEALTH MEASURE   47
4. THE SWEDISH REGIONALIZED HOSPITAL AND HEALTH SYSTEM   70

INDEX   87

# I

# HEALTH PLANNING IN A CHANGING SOCIETY

MY FIRST paper as a Heath Clark Lecturer was given the title Health Planning in a Changing Society for several reasons. Primarily, I felt that it is the rapid changes in the structure of a society where the progress of medicine and technology has reached a hitherto unknown explosive development that makes planning such an important and urgent activity of community life, not least as regards health and social welfare. Secondly, the title is meant to indicate the reasons for the choice of subjects of the following lectures and the context of the whole series.

## THE CHANGING SOCIETY

What changes does society present today? Which of them can be expected to involve special consequences for the planning of community health? When I point out some distinct changes this is because I personally feel that these factors have a specific and dominating influence on the philosophy of health planning. It should, however, be borne in mind that there is hardly any manifestation of modern social and economic life without influence in this respect. Planning for health must therefore always be integrated with socio-economic development planning.

This activity has, especially since the Second World War, emerged in many countries and has now spread throughout the world to the more advanced as well as to the developing nations. World-wide socio-economic development planning has been strongly promoted by the United Nations and the agencies related to the United Nations system. The nineteen-sixties have been designated as a United Nations Development Decade, and member states are urged to devote themselves to national development planning.

The 20th World Health Assembly (1967), in discussing Health and Economic Development, recalled that in many countries improvements in health conditions are not only desirable in themselves, but also essential for economic growth, and therefore they form an integral element in any meaningful development programme. The Assembly called the attention of members to the importance of taking appropriate steps to develop national health plans as part of their economic and social development plans, and reiterated the recommendation that governments should arrange appropriate representation of national health authorities in the national bodies established to plan and co-ordinate development programmes.

*Science* and *technology* are, of course, the most important transforming factors in the development of society at large. Industrialization and urbanization, have for centuries modified the structure of the community and constituted the fertile ground of the social revolution. The development of the communication system has more or less eliminated distances— no longer measured in time but in money—and brought all nations much closer to each other, and very much so as regards social and medical problems. Individuals feel more and more like world-citizens with a responsibility for their brothers everywhere. Modern medical science has always been regarded as an international concern but today every nation's medical activity has an international outlook that is becoming of increasing practical importance. There are hardly any longer any isolated, national health or social welfare problems.

We must be aware that medical science and technology will continue on a global scale and at an accelerated speed to provide the practice of medicine with new and more effective weapons against disease and disability. Every national health administration will in future feel more strongly the formidable pressure of implementing the results of medical and technological research in the practice of hygiene and medicine. More pathological conditions will be made accessible to treatment and more disability brought under compensatory control. This means a continuous demand for reorganization of the health services involving heavy investments. The history of medicine may tell us that this has always been the case. The difference is that today the process has reached such a speed that it is almost impossible to find trained personnel and material resources to follow up this development and its application as medical technology.

The processes of *industrialization* and *urbanization* are still progressively creating a society of more and more collectivism, where technical progress and all kinds of material and cultural resources, for good or evil, are easily at hand. This means that most individuals are brought under the mental and physical influence of modern life, mass-media and the impact of an artificial and synthetic environment.

*Family life* no longer means authority and protection and an atmosphere of peace, confidence and consolation. Both parents are often bread-winners. They marry young, there are more marriages than there were previously and divorce is more common. The children are therefore often taken care of in crèches, day nurseries or otherwise. Modern small but expensive flats no longer permit the family members to enjoy enough privacy. When the youngsters grow up and make a life of their own they do not find enough opportunity for freedom and independence at home and therefore they join the gang, go into the streets, to clubs, restaurants and so on. Family traditions are fading away. The contacts between the generations are superficial.

In our country especially, our experiences of narcotic drug addiction have taught us how strong an opposition there is against existing society—the establishment—from the side of youth. Young people have difficulty in explaining what changes they would like to see in society, they feel uneasy, isolated and do not see any real purpose of life. They are tempted to escape into alcoholism, narcotic abuse and juvenile delinquency. On the other hand their fight for individual freedom and against authority in addition to their demand for more education and an enriched cultural life is a stimulus to society.

Since the beginning of this century agriculture has continuously and substantially decreased its labour-force. This process has not yet stopped. In industry we have witnessed how *automation* has taken over manual work and the number of industrial workers has been cut down in spite of increasing production. In contradistinction, administrative and clerical staffs (salaried employees) of all ranks have increased. Quite recently there has been, in my country, a temporary standstill. The civil servants constitute one third of the increase of the total labour-force during the last 15 years.

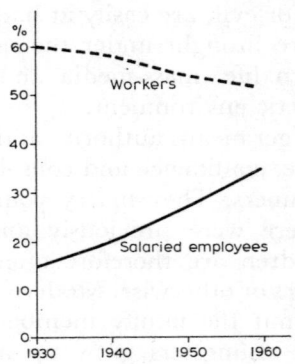

FIG. 1. Salaried employees and manual workers as a percentage of total active labour-force. (Source: Swedish National Census.)

*Working hours* have generally been cut down. Thus people can spend more time on their personal affairs including health. The *income per capita* has increased continuously and in Sweden today is the highest in Europe. The wealth of modern society and the abundance of free time are two factors contributing to the *affluence*, that seems so characteristic of our time.

There are no longer so many people needed to produce our food and whatever else belongs to the necessities of everyday life. Society is moving towards a state where *people are going to render each other services* as community officials or through private enterprise in an escalating manner. These services deal with all kinds of human activity—educational, cultural, social and health. Science, arts, technology and industry will, no doubt, be instrumental in introducing the tools for this service-rendering society, promising a richer, more imaginative existence to everybody. But these tools require operators—'service' people in the widest sense of the word. The hosts of teachers, of writers, and of people giving information through the mass-media (mainly on new facts and data which are so overwhelming to all of us) belong to this group. Another rapidly increasing service group is the category working in the big entertainment and tourist industry.

In my country we speak very correctly of the present explosive *epoch of education*. To illustrate this I would like to mention that the number of students at our universities was 21 000 in 1954, increased to 69 000 in 1965 and is expected to reach 90 000 in 1970. Reorganization of the primary and secondary schools, which are free, has made it easier for everybody to enter institutions of higher education.

Shortly the majority of the consumers of the health services of tomorrow will be well-educated and well-informed, service-rendering people who certainly do not hesitate to demand prompt ultra-modern service from our health agencies. What they want specifically, and that is not least the wish of the younger generation, is a *large amount of advisory and informative health service* in accordance with the tendency in other fields of the affluent society, but they also demand preventive measures including health control.

Let us not forget that youth is marching forward demanding a greater influence on social policy and the economy. As a consumer group they are, at least in my country, a dominating one thanks to high purchasing power and a widespread worship of affluence. This refers also to the health services.

Modern society with its emotional instability and materialism provides a challenge to the development of research in *psychiatry* and experimental psychology and to the study of *human ecology and ethology*. This is necessary if we are to be able to fill our lack of insight into the causation of human behaviour and to enable us to establish rationally the advisory and consultative health services the public needs in so many situations of life. This need is felt in particular by adolescents and their parents. All national health systems seem to be underdeveloped as regards child psychiatry. Hospital wards and most of all child and youth guidance clinics for ambulatory advisory activities are badly needed. Russian authors very often state that ephebiatrics is a neglected medical discipline and they are right in saying this. A close co-operation with the educational authorities to promote a constructive mental hygiene in all teaching institutions is highly desirable but lags behind. If we are to be able to master juvenile and adolescent misdemeanour and delinquency, to promote good social relationships and to loosen the strange motives for escape into alcohol, drugs and other means of 'intensive perception' into the artificial world of psychedelic philosophy, I feel we have to do something of this kind.

In the overcrowded collectivism of modern society with its overwhelming *communication possibilities* there are many lonely people who feel and suffer from their *loneliness*. This is particularly true of adolescents and old people.

Professor Hebb of Montreal and his group have studied the physiology of loneliness and demonstrated the deleterious effects of sensory deprivation. His experience seems to be relevant also for the noisy modern world where so many are feeling deprived of human warmth and direct individual contacts with the attendant flow of impressions stimulating to the mind. The health planner has to study research into loneliness.

It has also been claimed that the *stresses and strains of modern life*—the noisy hyperactivity, the restlessness, the harsh atmosphere of human relationships—are the causes of many mental disturbances and of psychosomatic diseases. We are certainly inclined to believe that this is true but there is hardly any really good evidence.

More obvious are such consequences of modern life as *accidents* (mainly traffic accidents) and *poisoning*. They represent a heavy load on our hospitals. Accidents are among the major causes of disability and therefore are of great social importance.

It has been said that modern technology creates more problems than it solves. Even if this is not true technical progress has greatly changed the ecology of man in a very dangerous sense. A state of imbalance between man and his natural surroundings has developed. Water, ground and air pollution are well-known health hazards which I do not

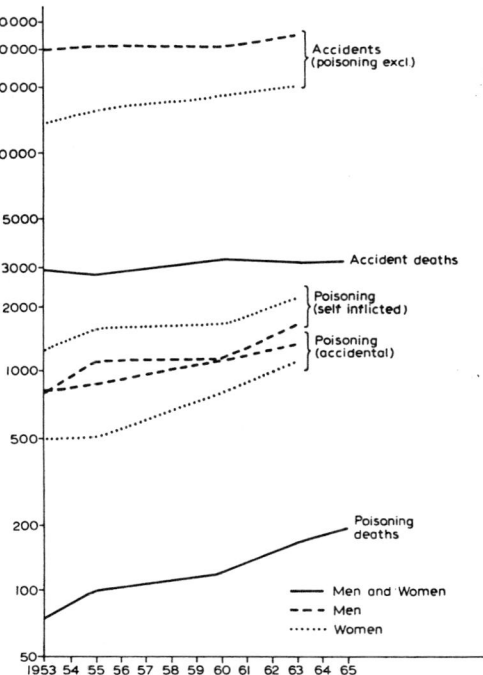

FIG. 2. Incidence of hospital admissions of accidents and poisoning by sex. Number of deaths from accidents and poisoning in hospital for both sexes together. Accidents (poisoning excluded) are a far more common cause of hospital admission and of death in hospital than poisoning. The incidence of poisoning is however increasing more rapidly. Logarithmic scale.

want to enter upon in particular. They offer remarkable and challenging examples of the role of chemical substances as causes of illness and death. Food technology has certainly rendered excellent services to health. On the other hand, the large number of food additives—in USA there are over 3000, in Sweden around 1000—could imply a potential danger. Toxicity especially in long-term use has not been adequately studied. In spite of the fact that additives undergo animal trials for toxicity before being accepted, we know that further studies have sometimes led to revised opinions.

Examples are phenetolcarbamide (sugar substitute) and nitrogen-trichloride (baking 'improving' additive to flour). The effect of biocides of all kinds in terms of long-term toxicity through intestinal resorption is not well known either in animals or in man. There is an urgent need for tolerance figures for man as regards food additives.

Toxicology is certainly a medical discipline in evolution. An international monitoring system seems to be as rightly indicated for toxic substances as for the adverse effects of drugs.

The Society of today is a highly drug-consuming one, and will be still more so tomorrow.

As a WHO-consultant I have together with Dr P. Siderius, Director-General of Health in the Netherlands, studied drug consumption in six European countries. This marks the interest of WHO in the health aspects of high drug consumption, which often takes the form of self-medication. The study has not yet been published.

I am, however, in a position to illustrate the increase of drug consumption in Sweden by showing the increase in prescriptions from 1939 to 1965.

The effect of the countless chemical substances surrounding the human organism will primarily manifest itself as toxic symptoms and signs of all kinds. It is to be foreseen that clinical toxicology will learn to recognize and treat them all. In Sweden a central agency called 'the poison information centre' at the Caroline Hospital in Stockholm is keeping a registry on chemical preparations used in everyday life and their composition. It gives information, mainly to the medical profession, on toxic ingredients and advice on treatment.

Chemicals may also induce allergies in man and there is no doubt that this group of diseases is increasing.

The third pathogenic effect is malignant neoplasias. In many countries cancer registries are functioning with the purpose of following changes in the incidence of different types and localization of cancer. Indications of carcinogenic effects of toxic substances in the environment can be achieved in this

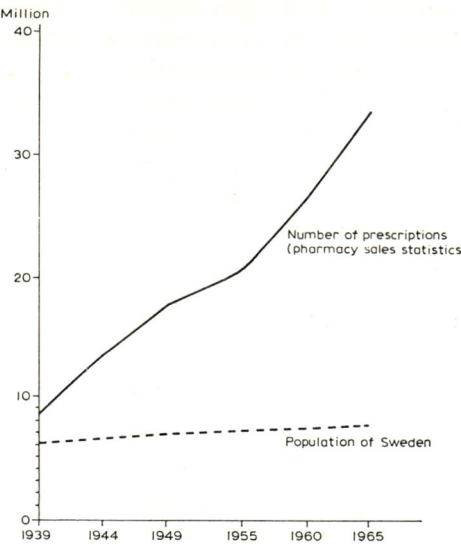

Fig. 3. According to the sales statistics of the Swedish pharmacies the number of prescriptions has markedly and continually increased. Since the compulsory health system with largely subsidized costs of prescribed drugs was introduced on 1 July 1955 the rise has been even more pronounced.

way. Air pollution and smoking in relation to cancer of the lung is one example. Personally, I am inclined to keep an eye on primary liver cancer, being myself extraordinarily suspicious of food additives.

The fourth effect of toxic substances could be said to be the teratogenic effect. Here again we have a warning system in our malformation registry which receives reports from all obstetric hospital departments every fortnight.

I have dwelt at some length on our *synthetic environment* and its health risks because I feel they will strongly influence the health of the people in the future and become of greater concern to the health administration than today.

The peaceful use of nuclear energy in modern society is

expected to increase. The health hazards of ionizing radiation were recognized early and protective measures were taken; apparently they have been very effective. There is every reason to believe that the situation will remain under control. Probably the risks from the mutagenic and carcinogenic effects of chemical substances mentioned earlier are higher.

*Modern society is an ageing one*—not least in Sweden where the birth rate is extremely low, 15·88 per thousand, and the expected life-span at birth is long—for women 75·45 and for men 71·49 years. The number of people over 70 years old corresponded to 6·4 per cent of our population in 1950. In 1960 the figure was 7·5 per cent and for 1970 and 1980 the estimates are 9·0 per cent and 10·9 per cent respectively. The aged person is a very high user of the health service.

There is a very marked increase in the use of medical care services by high-age-groups. The table on the next page[1] demonstrates this relationship by means of an index calculated from the use by age-groups of hospital facilities, other institutional care and medical consultations of all kinds.

This table demonstrates how the utilization of different kinds of medical care is distributed by ten year age-groups in relation to the total volume of care provided by the respective type of service. The last column shows these figures for all types of medical care together. A consumer unit is defined as one individual of the age-group representing the mean value for the use of health services by all age-groups. A person between 10 and 19 years of age represents half a unit. A person of about 50 is counted as one unit, and if seventy or more as two units.

No doubt our aging population will require a volume of medical care that is markedly high[2] and which health authorities should consider and plan for in time. The inequality of the demand for health services in different age-groups has brought

[1] Published 1961 by the commission for the study of the future needs of doctors (Chairman Dr A. Engel)

[2] Dr B. Smedby, Institute of Social Medicine, University of Uppsala, has informed me that according to his recent unpublished studies old people are using hospital facilities in a much higher degree than was found by the said commission in its inventory based on the year 1958.

HEALTH PLANNING IN A CHANGING SOCIETY

the Swedish National Board of Health to start operating with 'consumer units' in its planning instead of with the number of inhabitants.

TABLE 1. Health care usage by age groups, expressed as consumer units (see the text).

| Age | Number of consumer units in different ages | | | | |
|---|---|---|---|---|---|
| | General hospitals, TB and contagious diseases | Long term diseases | Mental diseases | Ambulatory care | Total |
| 0– 9 | 0·63 | 0·00 | 0·00 | 0·35 | 0·4 |
| 10–19 | 0·47 | 0·02 | 0·01 | 0·27 | 0·5 |
| 20–29 | 0·78 | 0·02 | 0·27 | 0·53 | 0·5 |
| 30–39 | 0·82 | 0·03 | 0·49 | 0·73 | 0·6 |
| 40–49 | 0·90 | 0·09 | 0·90 | 0·83 | 0·8 |
| 50–59 | 1·29 | 0·21 | 1·30 | 1·24 | 1·2 |
| 60–69 | 1·74 | 0·69 | 1·87 | 1·68 | 1·6 |
| 70–79 | 2·00 | 2·09 | 2·15 | 2·07 | 2·0 |
| 80– | 1·37 | 6·85 | 3·01 | 2·30 | 2·4 |

THE CHANGING PATTERN OF DISEASE AND DISABILITY. PUBLIC DEMAND FOR HEALTH SERVICES

The continuous changes inside modern society, the artificial, synthetic environment, the increasing resources and wealth have, of course, a great impact on *the pattern of disease* which has greatly been transformed. It is a pity that lack of morbidity statistics does not yet allow us to demonstrate this in an appropriate way; instead we have mostly to use mortality statistics.

The pattern of causes of death from different disease groups has greatly changed during the last 60 years as can be seen from Fig. 4. The decrease in death from infective diseases (not least TB) and the increase in cardiovascular diseases and malignant tumours are the most characteristic trends. Other observations of importance are the increased mortality from allergic and metabolic diseases. There is also a decrease in the diseases of the respiratory system. The decline of the curve at the bottom

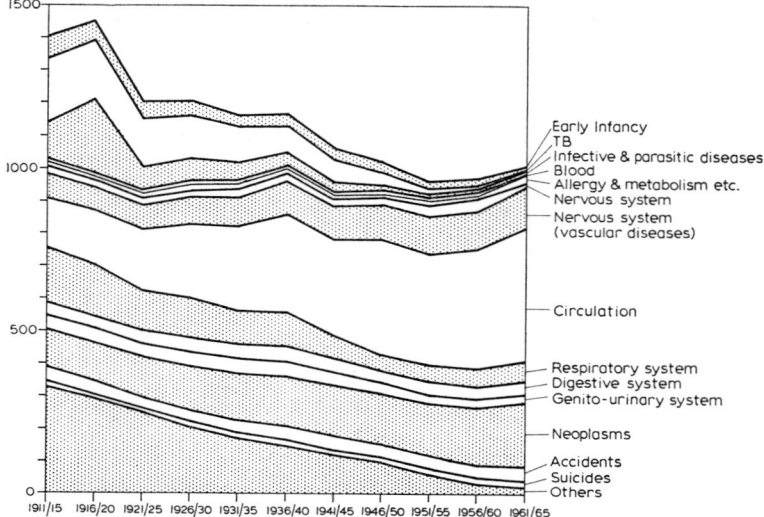

FIG. 4. Number of deaths per 100 000 of the Swedish population inside the most important disease classification groups (WHO) by average figures for each five-year period from 1911 onward. (Source: Swedish official mortality statistics.)

('other causes of death') is mainly a reflection of better diagnosis including more autopsies. The diagram illustrates where the main killing diseases are to be found today and how they have been taking over the role of the main killers of earlier days.

The most common diseases are, however, less serious conditions which are mainly treated outside the hospitals. I know very well that similar studies have been done in the United Kingdom but I nevertheless feel it would be of interest to refer to the Danish Morbidity Study of 1951 to 1953 (Table 2). This really tells you what people are suffering from in—if I may use the word—everyday life.

The results of modern medicine are considerably improving. More lives are saved, diseases previously inaccessible to medical treatment are now cured. Old age is no longer a contraindication to surgical intervention, many diseases like hypertension have got a much better prognosis but are not cured. Several respiratory diseases like pneumonia which formerly often led to death are today curable, at least in part, although sometimes resulting in some measure of respiratory incapacity. A similar situation exists for diseases of the kidney.

TABLE 2. The five leading disorders in the Danish population outside institutions

| Men | Women |
|---|---|
| Common cold | Common cold |
| Rheumatic disease, myalgia | Menstrual disturbance, gynaecological disorder |
| Chronic bronchitis | Rheumatic disease, myalgia |
| Disease of the digestive tract | Nervous and mental disease |
| Influenza | Chronic bronchitis |

There are no statistics available on disability that could inform us whether we are right in stating that there are more handicapped people in our society than formerly.

One thing, however, is evident, and this is that *disability* is more often recognized and no longer accepted with resignation as in the past. Medical technology is steadily providing better devices for the use of the disabled. I would remind the reader of the external power devices, of the use recently made of bio-electrical potentials to control prostheses and of other new inventions. These everybody agrees, should, regardless of costs, be supplied by the community. Speedy developments in this sector—as we have witnessed in regard to the rehabilitation of paralytic cases, to patients with cardiac and vascular diseases, renal failure and the hard of hearing etc.—will accelerate and will be able to compensate—often in combination with homotransplantation of tissues and organs.

To complete the panorama of disease and disability I would like to refer to a study by G. Lindgren and his collaborators on a Swedish health insurance population.

In 1962, Swedish health insurance legislation was amended and a very important statute introduced, namely that after 90 days of incapacity for work, the local insurance body has to investigate whether there are any reasons for undertaking extra rehabilitation measures. This could be said to be a control both of the patient and of his doctor in order to achieve the most rational treatment. It is not possible to go into details as regards the social and medical analysis of these so-called '90-day-cases' which was made in 1962 by a group of administrators and doctors belonging to the national health insurance of our four largest cities. What I would like to extract from this study are just a few findings to show that the number of 90-day-cases per thousand insured is ten times larger in the age-groups over 35 years than in the group 16–19 years. Furthermore, women are more represented than men and the dominance of the women is most pronounced in the younger age-groups.

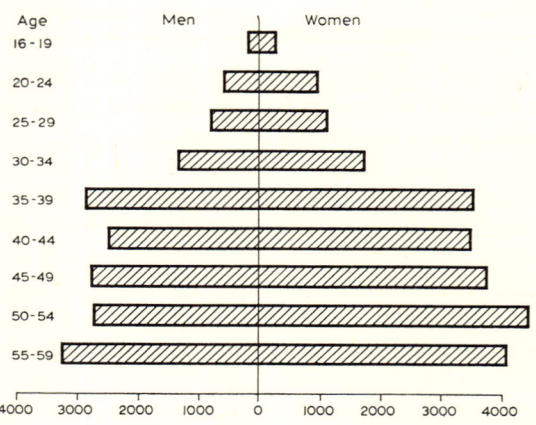

FIG. 5. Cases of 90 days' duration by age and sex.

The principal diseases from which these 90-day cases suffer are shown in Fig. 6 by diagnostic group and sex. The women are in a majority in all diagnostic groups, even accidents, with the exception of digestive ailments where men predominate, but not very much so.

Lastly Table 3 shows the distribution of the six most common diagnostic groups (three quarters of the total number of the 90-day-cases). The dominance of diseases of the bones and joints and of mental diseases should be underlined. This result has aroused an increased interest in the rehabilitation of diseases of the bones and joints and once again stresses the heavy burden of mental diseases.

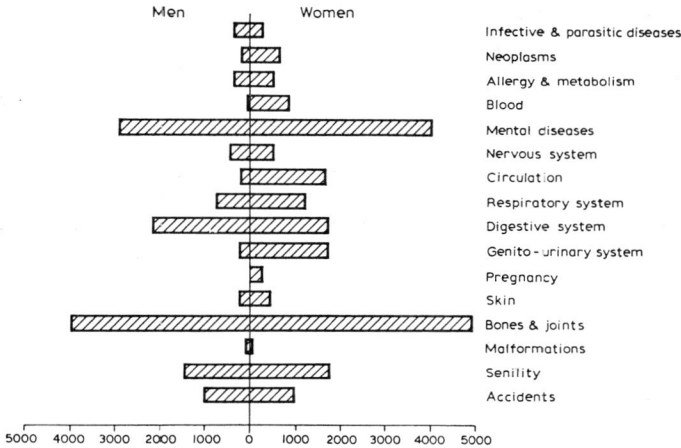

Fig. 6. Cases of 90 days' duration by diagnostic group and sex.

TABLE 3. Relative distribution of most common diagnoses of cases of 90 days' duration.

| Diagnostic group | Stockholm | Göteborg | Malmö | Norrköping |
|---|---|---|---|---|
| Mental | 17.9 | 22.1 | 17.4 | 16.5 |
| Circulatory | 8.3 | 7.3 | 6.8 | 10.2 |
| Digestive | 9.7 | 12.7 | 11.6 | 7.1 |
| Bones etc. | 21.4 | 29.1 | 22.8 | 30.2 |
| Senility | 10.6 | 1.4 | 13.0 | 7.9 |
| Accidents | 5.5 | 5.4 | 4.2 | 5.0 |
| Total | 73.4 | 78.0 | 75.8 | 76.9 |

The more explicitly modern pattern of disease would not get a complete presentation if I did not comment on psychiatric disease and mental retardation. All Swedish people disabled to the degree of two-thirds of what is regarded as normal working capacity can receive a disability pension during their 'active' period of life, that is from 16–67 years of age. The following figures illustrate the relative distribution of crippling health conditions among these pensioners. The very dominant role of the psychiatric cases should be observed.

16 HEALTH PLANNING IN A CHANGING SOCIETY

It is obvious that inborn errors of all kinds are the most prominent cause of disability among young people since the impact of poliomyelitis and tuberculosis has diminished. The great role of disability originating from prenatal, perinatal and even postnatal damage of the central nervous system must be carefully observed. The great number of youngsters with mental retardation, epilepsy and cerebral palsy, as well as other disorders of the nervous system of a metabolic or unknown character included here indicate a need for intensified research, which in due time may give us ways and means of preventing them.

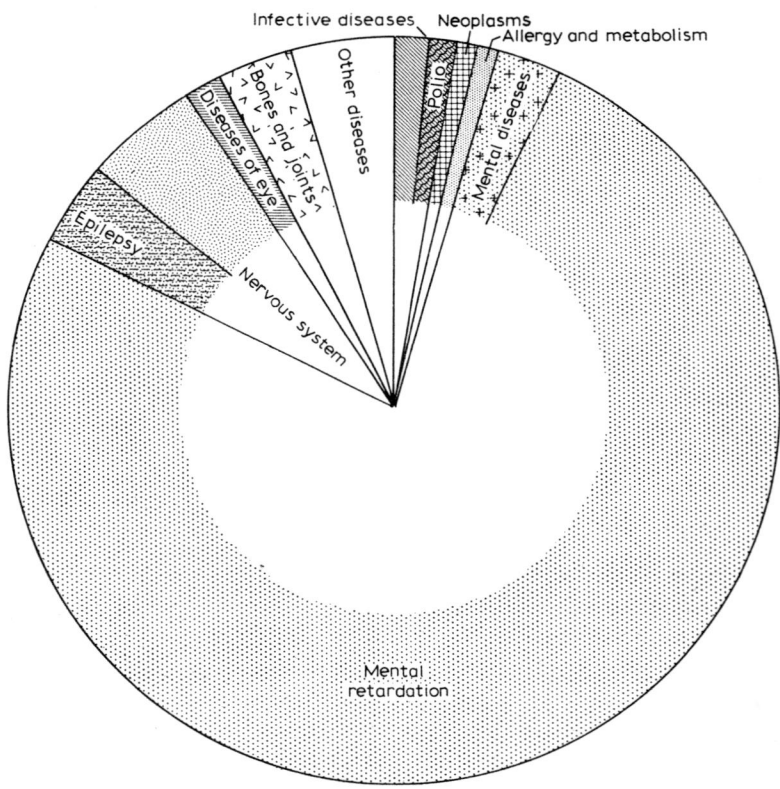

FIG. 7. Distribution of disability pensions by disease group. Age 16-19.

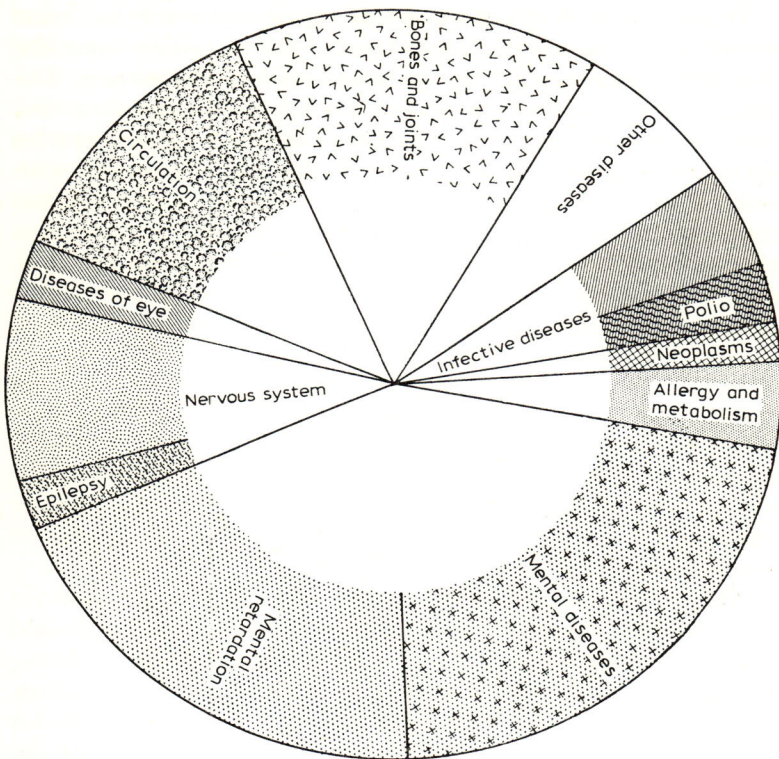

FIG. 8. Distribution of disability pensions by disease group. Age 16–66.

## HEALTH PLANNING ADAPTING

Having described some features of a modern society specifically relevant to health and presented a short review of the modern pattern of disease and disability I am going to discuss the repercussions on health planning.

What I will try to outline is a health policy for a modern society—an affluent well educated, service-rendering and service-demanding society with an ageing population—a society, having access to the achievements of medical and technological science in a state of evolution never witnessed before.

Beginning with the national health administration, I feel it will become of growing importance as the overall planning and innovating agency. It should be staffed for this purpose with people recruited from medical and technical research circles and with statisticians having modern electronic data-processing facilities. Representatives having social and economic knowledge and experience should join the integrated medical and social services which I consider to be of special importance to meet the needs of a modern society. In Sweden this integration came into operation at the top-level from 1st January, 1968 when the old Swedish National Board of Health was replaced by the new National Board of Health and Social Welfare.

More than in earlier days it is necessary for the leading health planner (i.e. the chief medical officer) to be in close touch with medical research. I myself have recently, when recommending a successor, expressed the opinion that the constructive imagination that is required from the top planner requires that he should be sought for among the ranks of research workers.

My experience in a small country has taught me that the responsibility for providing and running health services should be placed with regional and local authorities, who are living close to the problems and know the needs of the population. It has also been found easier to raise the necessary funds for health purposes at that level. The planning—I speak of the overall planning—should, however, be placed with the national health administration.

The hospital system will certainly undergo further rationalization. The larger hospitals will become more specialized in order to apply and develop the scientific progress of practical medicine. This is essential and pays off richly in all branches of preventive and curative medicine. Soon we will be aware of clinical genetics, immunology and toxicology marching in. These hospitals will contain computer departments for medical purposes including research and management. Much wider use of automated data-processing is to be expected over the whole health field.

Modern hospital care is always specialized care needing clinical departments and laboratories. Therefore, we should have no small hospitals—none with less than about 300 beds.

The smaller hospitals seem to face a very uncertain future. To illustrate my viewpoint on the development of medical care may I refer to a diagram showing the organization of hospital care and of public, extramural medical care in Sweden.

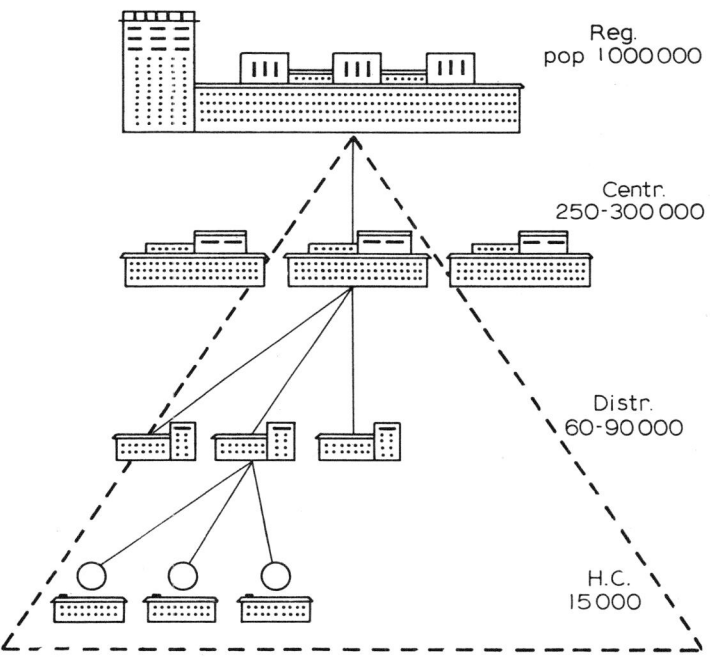

Fig. 9. Skeleton of the organization of the Swedish hospital system. Reg. = Regional hospital. Centr. = Central hospital (each county has one such hospital). Distr. = District hospital (formerly Normal hospital). H.C. = Health centre with attached peripheral nursing home. The figures refer to the approximate size of the catchment area. (Modified after S. Lindgren, in *Regional Hospital Planning*, valedictory volume dedicated to Arthur Engel; Nord. bokhandeln, Stockholm, 1967.)

At the top of the pyramid we find the regional hospital. It represents the intercounty level where 3–4 counties co-operate in providing the most specialized services. The catchment area is about 1 million people.

The succeeding levels are inside the counties. Each has its central hospital, highly specialized, but not offering the services of the 'superspecialties' to be represented at the regional level only.

I thus mean that regional hospitals (teaching or potential teaching hospitals) will expand, as will the central hospitals of the counties (on average 250 000–300 000 inhabitants). The district hospitals will get a larger catchment area (60 000–90 000 population). The smaller ones will be changed into homes for long-term care.

The number of hospital beds will probably increase very slightly in relation to the population increase. The growing geriatric clientèle should mainly be taken care of in nursing homes and similar institutions.

Health centres based on the local commune (municipality) are meant to provide a population of 10 000–20 000 with ambulatory preventive and curative care. These centres, still under development, are not part of the hospital organization, but our aim is to integrate their activities as closely as possible with the nearest district hospital. A goal not yet achieved anywhere is to have an exchange of medical personnel, primarily doctors, between the hospital and the health centres. May I add also that we nourish the hope of having our health centres staffed, in the future, with specialists in internal medicine, paediatrics, obstetrics and gynaecology, and psychiatry, and with a doctor of social medicine as a co-ordinator and leader. This would mean a more effective pattern of medical practice.

This is the level where most of the advisory services I spoke of earlier are to be rendered.

The chief of the National Board of Health Division for the Care of the Mentally Retarded, Dr K. Grunewald, claims that the activities of the paediatricians should be devoted much more to preventive measures, including educational and advisory services for children, young people and their parents, and to the rehabilitation of the disabled. He also recommends health control of children and adolescents starting at the classical mother and child welfare clinic and finishing with health supervision at schools and universities. He wants a new type of paediatrician trained for all these functions, that is, a doctor capable of meeting the demands of the new society. Certainly he needs a considerable education and training in psychology and child psychiatry.

Psychiatry and child psychiatry in particular, must be developed and made to co-operate very closely with other branches inside the hospitals. The existing isolated mental hospitals are to be used for chronic cases only and mainly for geriatric patients. The borderland between psychiatry and internal medicine and other disciplines should be worked out not least for the study of psychosomatic medicine and its socio-medical aspects.

Psychiatric services at all levels are essential for the development of the individual advisory services I have already mentioned, but not least to help forward better human relations in modern society.

Physical and mental disability in general will be much more looked after. Modern technology will provide us steadily with more developed services to eliminate all kinds of disability. Our Government's commitment to the problems and suffering of the disabled is today very deep and strong and will be met by a rehabilitation programme that will know no limitations of costs.

Environmental hygiene in the wide ecological sense will be developed and better methods of following changes will be sought, especially as regards mental health and the chemical environment.

Modern medicine with its strong influx of technology, sociology and psychology and its orientation towards more advisory, preventive and social activities has to embark upon a wide range of new training programmes, many of them having an entirely new content. Very often they will offer a combined medical, technological, biological, psychological and socioeconomic education. I feel it is in this way that medical manpower has to be equipped. This a matter of urgency.

There are great difficulties in taking care of the aged in their homes or in the homes of relatives. Modern housing and the occupationally active housewife are factors that do not favour such care. We therefore estimate that institutional care (mainly in nursing homes) will be necessary for no less than 55 per thousand of all people over 70 years of age.

As the care of the aged is such an immense problem in modern society and as in many countries, there, are too few young people to take care of them, I will, give a glimpse of our system by means of a scheme (Fig. 10).

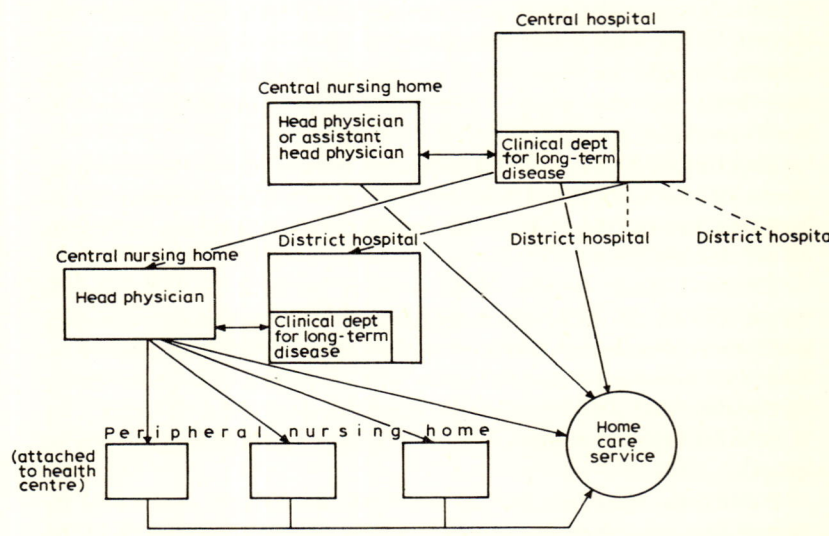

FIG. 10. Organization of long-term medical care in Sweden. There are three different functional levels. The department for long-term diseases of the central and district hospitals is primarily practising an assessment function. The central nursing homes mainly offer rehabilitation and the peripheral homes in principle long-term care. Of course there is at all levels an integration of these functions.

I would like to underline especially the importance of constructing nursing homes with good rehabilitation facilities for the increasing number of elderly people with long-term illness or disability.

While I feel it is necessary for reasons of economy and medical manpower to be cautious in expanding the volume of hospital care, yet specialization within the existing situation should be considered and also the promotion of clinical research. Investments in one hospital bed amount to £22 500 (310 000 Sw.cr.) and the running cost per day per bed went up in 1966 to nearly £15 in the regional, teaching hospitals and to £11 for all hospitals (average figure). These costs should be compared with building costs and running costs in nursing homes roughly amounting to £420 and £4, respectively.[1]

There is competition from many other activities in any society that demands increased investments and additional labour force. The economic point of view should not be overlooked by the health planner. An intelligent control of the automatic growth of the health services is necessary if the health sector is to be able, not only to maintain, but to motivate an enlargement of its share in the gross national product.[2] With the enormously rising costs of hospital building and of hospital operation, carefully rationalized hospital planning inside a comprehensive system of health and social care is of the utmost importance. More emphasis must be put on the development of the less expensive hospital out-patient departments and health agencies outside the hospitals. Ambulatory and domiciliary care based on local doctors and their staffs, operating from health centres, must be given a high priority, as well as nursing homes and rehabilitation agencies primarily for the elderly etc. From these facilities will emanate the educational, advisory and preventive services so close to the mind of the modern sophisticated, service-rendering and affluent society.

Modern people are interested in all preventive measures and are requesting from the health authorities the resources to remain healthy and to have their health condition checked from time to time to reveal disease at an early stage, preferably in the asymptomatic stage. They are going to ask for personal medical advice in an increasing number of situations of life. Health—partly thanks to the insurance system—is looked upon as a citizen's right.

With this approach medicine and social welfare can no longer be separated as community activities. In Sweden, we are therefore, as I said earlier, integrating those services. This

[1] £1 = 15 Sw. cr. (Oct. 1967)
[2] This share was 5·7 per cent in Sweden in the year 1965.

means that the medical practice of tomorrow will comprise much more social medicine and much more psychology and psychiatry. Increasing investments in medical, psychological and sociological research should be foreseen. Governments will realize that this means exercising preventive medicine in its highest potency, the key to a better health and a more dignified life in a turbulent epoch.

## REFERENCES

CLEMEDSON, C.-J. (1965) Vår syntetiska miljö som hälsovårdsproblem (Our synthetic environment as a health problem). *Läkartidningen* 62, 2115.
DUBOS, R. (1967) *Man Adapting*. New Haven and London: Yale University Press.
ENGEL, A. (1965) Health planning in a changing society. *World Hospitals* 1, 255.
ENGEL, A. (1965) Uppfordran till forskning över psykisk utvecklingsstörning (A challenge to research in mental retardation). *Nord. Med.* 73, 313.
ENGEL, A. (1962) The Swedish regionalized Hospital System. *First Conference on Hospital Services of Western Europe*, p. 248. London: King Edward's Hospital Fund for London.
GRUNEWALD, K. (1966) Morgondagens barnläkare (The Paediatrician of Tomorrow). *Läkartidningen* 63, 2222.
HEBB, D. O. (1961) Sensory Deprivation. *J. Nerv. & Ment. Dis.* 132, 40.
LERNER, M. and ANDERSSON, O. W. (1963) *Health Progress in the United States 1900–1960*. Chicago & London: The University of Chicago Press.
LINDGREN and COLL. (1965) Långtidssjuka i våra storstäder 1962 (Chronic Illness in Sweden's four largest cities). *Soc. med. tidskrift*, Suppl. 32.
LINDGREN, S. (1967) 'Yesterday-Today-Tomorrow' in *Regional Hospital Planning* edited by Tottie & Janzon. Stockholm: Nordiska bokhandeln.
LINDHARDT (1960) *Sygdomsundersogelsen i Danmark 1931–1954*. Copenhagen: Munksgaard.
MASSE, P. (1965) *Le plan ou l'anti-hasard*. Paris: Gallimard
VILLEY, R. (1966) *Reflexion sur la medicine d'hier et de demain*. Paris: Plon.
WATERSTON, A. (1965) *Development Planning*. Baltimore Md: The Johns Hopkins Press.
COMMISSION ON CHRONIC ILLNESS (1957) *Chronic illness in a large city*, vol. 4. Cambridge, Mass: Harvard University.
COMMISSION ON CHRONIC ILLNESS (1959) *Chronic illness in a rural area*, vol. 3. Ibid.

# HEALTH PLANNING IN A CHANGING SOCIETY

OFFICIAL STATISTICS OF SWEDEN:

*Causes of death. Annual Report of the Central Bureau of Statistics.* (1911–65) Stockholm: Statistiska Centralbyrån.

*Census of Population in 1950 and 1960.* Stockholm: Statistiska Centralbyrån (The Central Bureau of Statistics).

*National Insurance. Annual Report of The National Insurance Board.* (1961) Stockholm: Statistiska Centralbyrån (The Central Bureau of Statistics).

*Public Health. Annual Report of the National Board of Health.* (1952–65) Stockholm: Kungliga Medicinalstyrelsen.

REPORTS:

*Sjukhusens förvaltningsekonomiska statistik för år 1966 (Administrative and economic hospital statistics for the year 1966).* (1967) Stockholm: Kungliga Medicinalstyrelsen (National Board of Health).

*Nationalräkenskaper (National Accounts) 1950–1966.* (1967) Stockholm: Statistiska Centralbyrån (National Central Bureau for Statistics).

*S.O.U. (Swedish Government Official Reports)* 1961, **8**. (1961) Government Commission on the future Need of Doctors. Stockholm: Inrikesdepartementet (Home Office).

*S.O.U. (Swedish Government Official Reports)* 1967, **25** and **41**. (1967) Government Commission on the Problem of Narcotic Addiction. Stockholm: Socialdepartementet (Ministry for Social Affairs).

*Official records of the World Health Organization* No. 160 Twentieth World Health Assembly Part I (1967). Geneva: WHO.

## 2

## STATISTICS AND HEALTH PLANNING

IN MY first lecture I mentioned statistical information as a main guide to the health planner. It is surprising that this very simple statement, today repeated almost monotonously, did not meet with approval and achieve practical implementation in health planning until quite recently—say during the last 10 to 15 years.

Earlier the planner worked rather tentatively. If a need for health facilities was experienced he was rarely taking the risk of overloading the resources and therefore made no attempt to find a quantitative expression of this need. No serious efforts were made to find an optimal distribution of the services so as to get a maximum of the inhabitants of a community conveniently served. The influence of a powerful local politician or an active local press, and even the residence of a private donor, many times decided where to place a new health institution. The skill and reputation of a hospital staff or even of a single prominent medical staff member have many times—and often rightly so—been responsible for the development of a specific hospital. But it was rarely considered whether these valuable resources of personnel could have been better used in new hospital departments elsewhere to the greater benefit of the community as a whole.

The necessity of making the best use of our accumulated resources of investments and manpower, trained or available for training, has now finally forced most countries to enter upon well documented rational health planning and this means, not least, better health statistics. Where public authorities were responsible for the care of the sick and for the promotion of health this planning was initiated early. Where there existed a voluntary health system it was postponed.

In spite of leading achievements in health statistics the application of this information in an area-wide hospital plan is of very recent date—for example in the United States. Federal regulations on regional health planning were only enacted at the end of 1966.

What statistics are thought to be of a special value in planning for health? In fact they are manifold. Most of them have to be collected continuously as routine statistics, others *ad hoc* or on a trial basis.

### DEMOGRAPHIC AND VITAL STATISTICS

Current statistics should give full information on the population, the changes in its size and composition by age, sex and race, the geographical distribution, status of urbanization, occupation and income per capita. These vital or demographic statistics are as a rule not prepared by health authorities but by national statistical agencies. They include, however, some fundamental information on the health standard of a nation viz. infant mortality, maternity mortality and expectation of life. I personally feel these figures probably are the best expression of the health condition of a country and the efficiency of its health services.

For the health planner it is also important to be on the lookout for population migration, which nowadays occurs with a great rapidity and demands prompt adaptation of the services. The effect of the migration can be rather disastrous for the health authorities when the migrants, as in rural districts, are recruited mostly among the younger age-groups. Too many old people are left in great need of medical care but not enough young people are available to give that care.

In many Swedish areas the health system has had to be reorganized to deal with this situation. The main remedy has been more nursing homes and the strengthening of the resources for domiciliary care. At the same time as the need for geriatric care is met on essential points, the shortage of doctors and nurses and of a young labour force in general can be more easily overcome.

In order to illustrate the importance of vital statistics I should like to give a further example. The mortality during the first year of life compared with the first month, week and day of life respectively shows very marked differences. The rapid decrease of total infant mortality has not been followed by a corresponding decrease during the immediate postnatal period. The curve

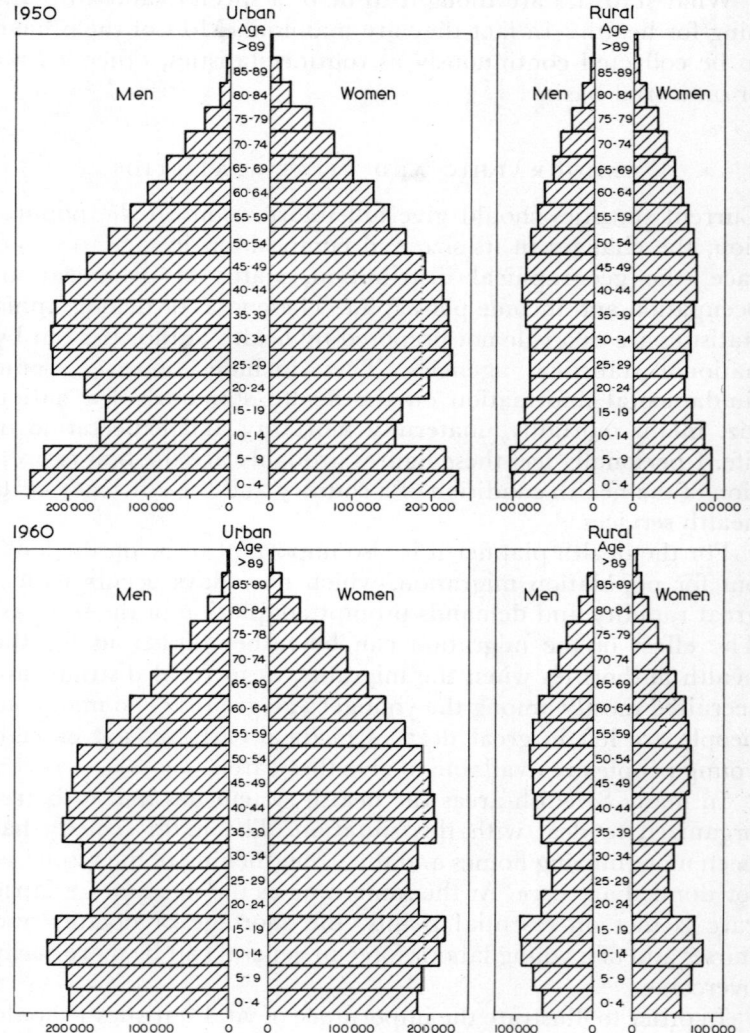

FIG. 11. National Census in Sweden 1950 and 1960. Population distribution by age in urban and rural areas. Absolute figures.

of the stillborn was also for a long time quite stable as can be seen from the diagram (Fig. 12) but from 1940 onwards there was a steady decrease in the number of stillbirths. The main causes for this change are, in the first place, the increasing number of deliveries in specialized hospital departments guaranteeing better obstetrical care. Improved socio-economic living conditions have, also, largely contributed.

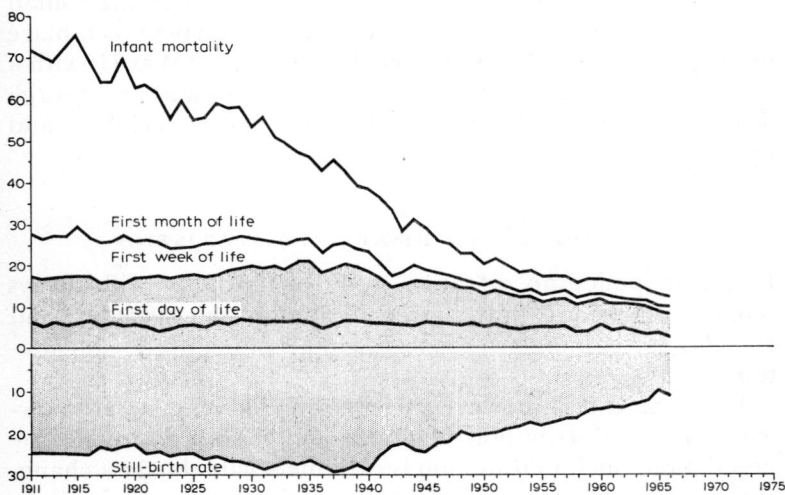

FIG. 12. Still-birth rate and infant mortality per 1000 of population 1911–66.

The difficulties of medical care in reducing substantially postnatal mortality has brought forward comprehensive studies to elucidate the reasons for this failure. WHO organized a series of expert committees and conferences to study the problem. This provided an impetus to promote prenatal and perinatal research and embryo-anatomy but also resulted in practical organizational measures aiming at a broader co-operation between obstetric and paediatric services. Studies in obstetrical techniques and in the care of the premature child were also stimulated, as was the care of the pregnant woman. Gregg's observation of the role of rubeola and Lenz's of the teratogenic effect of thalidomide added a great deal to the increasing interest in prenatal research and prenatal care. The practical results of all this are quantitatively modest but nevertheless of great importance. Bearing in mind that early infant mortality is mainly caused by pulmonary abnormalities (hyaline membranes) and malformations and that we know very little about the etiology of these conditions this is not surprising.[1]

The statistics of *causes of death* were until recently our only guide for getting an impression of the pattern of disease. Notifiable diseases were, however, an exception covering a small field only. Everybody knows the changes that have taken place in the panorama of disease especially since World War II, with a reduction of mortality from infectious diseases and an upsurge of deaths from cardiovascular diseases, cancer, accidents and poisoning.

### MORBIDITY AND DISABILITY STATISTICS

In health policy an attentive study of mortality will always remain important but statistical studies on *morbidity* and *disability* are gaining ground as essentials of health documentation.

It is a hard task, however, to obtain reliable, general knowledge of the distribution of illness and disability among the population. Such information is extremely valuable in a changing society where *continuous watch on the health situation* is so strongly indicated. It should be organized so as to *serve as a monitoring system* to signal new health situations and hazards and to expose defects in environmental sanitation, medical care and rehabilitation. Such statistics would thus serve as a watchdog of the national health administration and constitute a basis for readjustments and new activities.

There are several ways of reaching this type of information.

(1) Where a compulsory *national health insurance system* exists information should be collected from its statistical files. In Sweden as in other countries, I assume, there are great difficul-

---

[1] Many publications of recent years are a definite expression of the growing interest in the development of the lung, its anatomy and the regressive changes in the ageing individual. All represent a recognition of the major role of this organ in the first and in the terminal phase of human life. Third ranking cause of stillbirth in Sweden is erythroblastosis.

ties in obtaining reliable and full information on the nature of diseases and injuries from this source.

In Sweden, a doctor's certificate is required from the sixth day after the sickness was reported to the insurance authorities. This means that the majority of short-term illnesses remain unregistered. The medical certificates, very often and quite understandably, contain a symptomatic diagnosis or just the information that for the time being none could be made. Furthermore, even a plain diagnosis can be doubted, for example because of limited diagnostic resources. There are also other biases connected with the insurance material. Children under 16 years of age and adults over 67 are not included—both groups of significant weight in health planning matters. Minor illnesses without incapacity for work are, of course, not reported to the insurance offices.

Statistics from health insurance have, of course, been used for several *ad hoc* studies, for example in my country on the causes of diseases among people incapacitated for work for more than three months (Lindgren and collaborators) and on drug consumption (Smedby, Swarén).

(2) Investigation of a representative *sample of the population*. This method has been used since the turn of the century (Charles Booth in 'Labour and Life in London, 1889–1903'). Of course, there are many procedures; forms to be filled in by the public; household inquiries by trained or untrained interviewers, *ad hoc* or covering a longer period as for example the Danish Morbidity Study 1951–3, where one per thousand of the population over 15 years of age was interviewed every month for three years by trained interviewers. The interviews were individual in contradistinction to the more common household (panel) interviews. The Danish investigation is a very informative one especially as regards minor diseases.

I think it is of interest to see a list of the most common diseases among the Danish population (Table 4).

(3) The *continuous population sample* is a new technique of collecting statistics that is valuable for the health administration, especially when urgent information is required on a specific problem. To check the function of existing health systems, to assess changing needs of health care, to detect new health

hazards it is a great advantage to have at hand a fixed sample for inquiry or examination.

TABLE 4. The five leading disorders in the Danish population outside institutions.

| Men | Women |
| --- | --- |
| Common cold | Common cold |
| Rheumatic disease, myalgia | Menstrual disturbance, gynaecological disorder |
| Chronic bronchitis | Rheumatic disease, myalgia |
| Disease of the digestive tract | Nervous and mental disease |
| Influenza | Chronic bronchitis |

The selection and maintenance of the sample is, of course, of paramount importance.

The sample should be a probability one. Valuable results can be obtained through studies of selected population groups inside the sample. In its design full use must be made of the various techniques to increase its efficiency, such as stratification, clustering, etc.

Care must be taken to ensure that the sample is adequate in respect of background variables. For example, environment is an important factor in epidemiology, and if the statistics are to illustrate the spread of disease it is essential to have a sufficient geographic distribution of the sample. It should be stratified to show the type of community, rural or urban, proximity to medical resources of various kinds, and so on, as well as the age and sex of those in the sample. According to the type of data required, certain categories can be over-represented in the sample drawn on a particular occasion, as for instance when it is desired to ask questions concerning health in old age.

Sometimes it is possible to use only certain groups in the sample, schoolchildren for example. From the statistical point of view this may be unsatisfactory, but it may be worthwhile as a means of getting some indications which can then be further investigated. Geographical coverage in a field survey is a controversial question, as we have usually to consider not only what is theoretically desirable but what is practically possible within the limits of resources available.

## STATISTICS AND HEALTH PLANNING

The idea of a fixed sample for continuous questioning is attractive, because the initial cost of setting it up would burden a series of surveys only once to its full extent, and subsequently costs would be at a minimum and collection would be easier. Unfortunately, such a sample would soon have a distorting effect on the data. Those in the sample would soon become tired of answering questions, or their responses might be affected by the knowledge that they are members of a sample. This could to some extent be avoided by either *rotating the sample*, so that a part only is used each time, and only after a relatively long interval is any individual interviewed again, or by replacing part of the sample on each occasion by a new part. However, one of the most difficult problems remains: that of ensuring by some system of up-dating that over a period of time the changes taking place in the whole population are reflected in the selected sample.

A good sampling procedure becomes worthless if the instrument used to collect the data is defective. The questions must be carefully prepared and tested in detail before use and some control questions should be included for continuous data quality control. Investigators need training in the interview technique, but though they need sufficient medical knowledge for the purpose of the survey they are engaged upon, the evidence available indicates that trained amateur interviewers seem to get results equivalent to those from medically trained people in most instances. If there is an organization to undertake field investigations, this should be used so as to keep the costs down, and only a short period of special training will be necessary.

A Swedish continuous population sample is that consisting of *all individuals aged 16 to 67 years and born on 15 February* (i.e. one three-hundred-and-sixty-fifth of the total population) with a random geographical distribution (popularly called the 15th borns). This tool has been used for the purpose of getting a picture of morbidity in the population. to study the use of different health facilities, the cost of illness, drug consumption, etc. District nurses have been widely used as interviewers.

The United States National Health Survey is a well-known example of the use of a continuous sample of households, interviewed weekly and so selected that the week's interviews represent a random sample of the entire population.

For more information on health surveys using this method I wish to refer to the World Health Organization, Regional Office for Europe (1967) Continucus Health Surveys of the Population, Report, Copenhagen (EURO 215(3)/5).

(4) The art and practice of hospital diagnoses must be said to be of a very high standard and can therefore serve as a reliable source of information on the pattern of morbidity of that part of the population that has been hospitalized for examination or treatment. This population represents a relatively small group but a group of extraordinary importance for hospital planning especially on a large scale.

In 1962 the National Board of Health started to collect individual data on patients on discharge from mental hospitals and psychiatric departments of general hospitals. In 1964 these statistics were extended to cover *all* hospitals and nursing homes for physical diseases inside the Uppsala hospital region (one of the seven Swedish hospital regions) and the city of Malmö in the South of Sweden. Births taking place in the same hospitals were also included in the study.

The purpose of *hospital morbidity statistics* is to give information on the causes of hospitalization and—in the long run—on changes in the specific pattern of disease, on length of stay and on the sex and age distribution of the hospital population. Such data can serve as a basis for planning the hospital services. They are also meant to be a basis for research and to serve as a frame for sample surveys of different kinds. The data are fed back to the hospitals to serve as a diagnostic register etc. (Fig. 13).

Data are submitted by the separate hospital departments on two types of form, one of which refers to the newborn. The medical officer in charge is responsible for reporting. Hospital doctors complained earlier of *the WHO* four digit *Classification of Diseases*, which had to be used. It was thought that it limited the possibility of registering more specific diagnoses which were valuable from the clinical scientific point of view. Since we introduced *five digits* they seem to be much more satisfied.

The forms are submitted regularly every fortnight to the National Board of Health; they are, in principle, self-coding but subject to assessment in the statistical department, particularly as regards notes on diagnoses and operations, deliveries etc. which are scrutinized by physicians.

With the present extent of the project, the yearly number of forms to be taken care of is estimated at about 200 000.

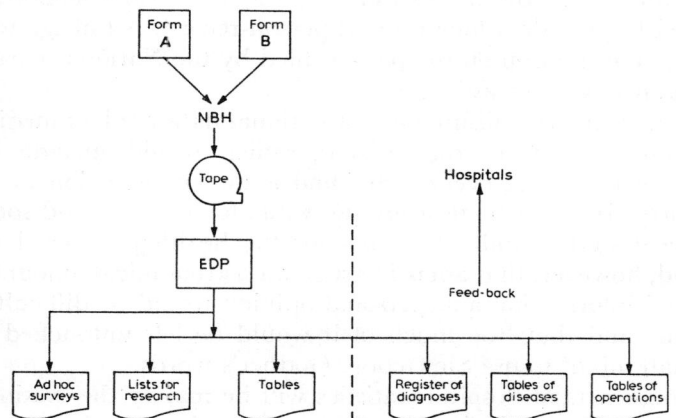

FIG. 13. Hospital morbidity statistics procedure. A = all patients except the newborn. B = newborn. NBH = National Board of Health (Statistical division). EDP = Electronic data processing.

The automatic processing of the material is done through Electronic Data Processing. According to the plan, as a feedback, lists and tables are produced for each hospital department, showing the patients with all relevant data arranged after diagnoses. Such lists are then handed over to the departments to be used by them as diagnostic indices. For departments doing surgery a consolidated list showing the operations is also compiled. Further, a list for the whole area is produced giving the cases in the first line by diagnoses. This list is intended as a source for research work.

The form is so constructed that the identification of the individual must be done through an identity number (and case paper number) alone.

This identity number is the civil registration number, composed of the date of birth expressed by the two last figures of the year of birth, the month and the day both containing two figures and a serial number inside the population group born the same day, odd for men and even for women. My own identity number is thus 00/09/17/715.

To have the whole population registered in this way opens up great advantages. The statistical hospital case reports always contain the identity number of the patient and can therefore be linked to provide a longitudinal person-record. A linkage with all the information on the patient filed by the National Health Insurance is also feasible.

In fact, the establishment of a national data bank of medical life-time records of the citizens, which would include the medical history of every individual is under discussion in my country. It could be of a unique value for medical and sociomedical studies and surely also for the health planner. I am afraid, however, that amassing such an astronomical amount of factual information and personal opinion would be difficult to handle and that 'too much of it would be left untouched by human mind' to use Sir George Godber's words.

Consumers of hospital statistics will be mainly the National Board of Health in its capacity as supervising and planning body, the county councils, the hospitals themselves, the National Insurance Board, *ad hoc* committees on questions of health and sickness, research workers and not least, co-operating agencies abroad.

Consultations with representatives from Denmark and Finland have taken place with a view to co-ordinating the statistical aims in the three countries.

In the future one can envisage co-ordination with the statistics of the National Insurance Board dealing with the sickness insurance services. This would make a display of the complete sickness periods for different diagnoses possible.

Another question which may be raised in this connexion is the follow-up of mass health examinations. The morbidity statistics might also be useful for checking the representativeness of, for instance, statistics on causes of death and of the cancer register.

(5) *Disability statistics.* Nowadays many patients who would previously have died of their disease are saved, their health condition is ameliorated but an anatomical or functional

disability may often persist. I am referring in particular to respiratory and heart diseases, neurological disorders and renal failure. It must also be realized that the result of treatment in the higher-age-groups very often does not end in a *restitutio ad integrum*.

What has been said of diseases is also true of injuries and very markedly so of the modern treatment of injuries to the brain and spinal cord, frequently caused by traffic accidents.

We have certainly to expect—in spite of the disappearance of polio—an increasing number of disabled people whom we must be able to take care of, rehabilitate and provide with more and more advanced technical devices. In my opinion there will be very few handicapped in the future who cannot be restored to a tolerable social life. There is, however, one group where our efforts will I fear mostly fail in this respect viz. the mentally retarded.

Under all circumstances a better knowledge of disability is required. As I see it hospitals should report on temporary or persistent disability at the discharge of the patient.

The Swedish Health Insurance produces annual *statistics on the pensions allocated to disabled people between 16 and 66 years*. This has for long time been our most reliable source of information of this kind. It includes high degrees of handicaps only.

Figs 7 and 8 (pages 16–17) show the distribution of different types of disability, one referring to age-group 16 to 19 years and the other to all who have received a 'disability pension' which is paid to everybody between 16 and 66 years of age who because of a disability is not expected to make his own living. Thereafter the old age pension system comes into operation. The role of the diseases of bones and joints, heart failure and neurological disorders as crippling factors are well known, but perhaps not so the predominance of mental retardation and mental diseases. It should be noted that at the age when young people are about to enter productive life the most common cause of disability (87 per cent of the total number of pensioners) is mental retardation and allied CNS-damage, acquired, prenatal, perinatal or during the first years of life.

## HEALTH SERVICES ACTIVITY STATISTICS

These statistics have for a long time been developed in the hospital field on administrative and economic lines giving the number of admissions, length of stay, deaths as well as running costs, etc. They exist side by side with medical statistics giving the number and nature of diseases and injuries treated and reporting the most important therapeutic and diagnostic measures such as operations, anaesthetics and radiology.

The full implementation of both these components will not be achieved until we have found a method of co-ordinating them in an *evaluation of the services*, including clear statements on the medical achievements and on the specified costs related to them. A more complete classification of medical procedures is required, which will permit us to estimate or appraise the results of hospital activities. We are only in the beginning of an attempt to create better and more differentiated expressions for the results of treatment than the routine recording on the discharge of the patient of 'improved', 'not improved' or 'dead'.

Routine statistics on the activities of district doctors (medical officers), district nurses (public health nurses) and midwives, covering maternity and child health services, vaccinations and inoculations, consultation bureaux for family planning and consultation centres for child and youth psychiatry are in my country considered to be a worthwhile means of keeping in touch with a wide range of social and medical problems.

As regards ambulatory medical care, in Sweden half of the total number of patients are taken care of by the outpatient departments of the hospitals. The other half is more or less equally divided between the district doctors and the general practitioners. The number of consultations is recorded. The latter group (mainly active in the big cities) does not issue any reports. For the time being we do not think there is any reason for requiring more detailed reports. More medical information of value could, however, be collected from the outpatient departments elucidating the panorama of minor diseases and injuries.

## STATISTICS ON MEDICAL CARE FACILITIES AND OTHER HEALTH RESOURCES

This type of statistics is naturally worked out by the responsible regional and local authorities and presented to the central administration. I have here only a few remarks. Primarily, I feel these statistical reports should also cover the field of social welfare, realizing that there is a broad borderland between these two activities and integration is therefore needed.

Secondly, I should like to mention that we in Sweden have tried to combine the routine statistics on resources with the information obtained from local authorities on the expected development of the services during the next five year period, according to existing plans. How successful this will be I do not know yet.

Another procedure that is I think rather unusual is the custom of the Swedish National Board of Health to inquire occasionally about the bed situation in hospitals. This is done chiefly in the summer from June 1 to August 31 when many wards are closed because of shortage of personnel, or for annual repair and intensive cleaning. The latter provides a link in the campaign for the prevention of hospital infections. It should be noted that about one third of the beds of the general hospitals can be closed during this season without increase of the bed occupancy rates (Fig. 14).

## STATISTICS ON HEALTH PERSONNEL

For many years the Swedish health services have been operating under conditions of understaffing because of shortage of doctors, nurses, physiotherapists and practically all groups within the health labour force. This has brought forward the setting up of complete registers of all medical and paramedical personnel—address, education and training, previous and present posts, etc. Notification of changes are submitted continuously but particularly in connexion with *the annual reports that all trained medical personnel are obliged to present.* These registers serve as a basis for the calculation of the supply of personnel and their expected availability for active service in general or in certain

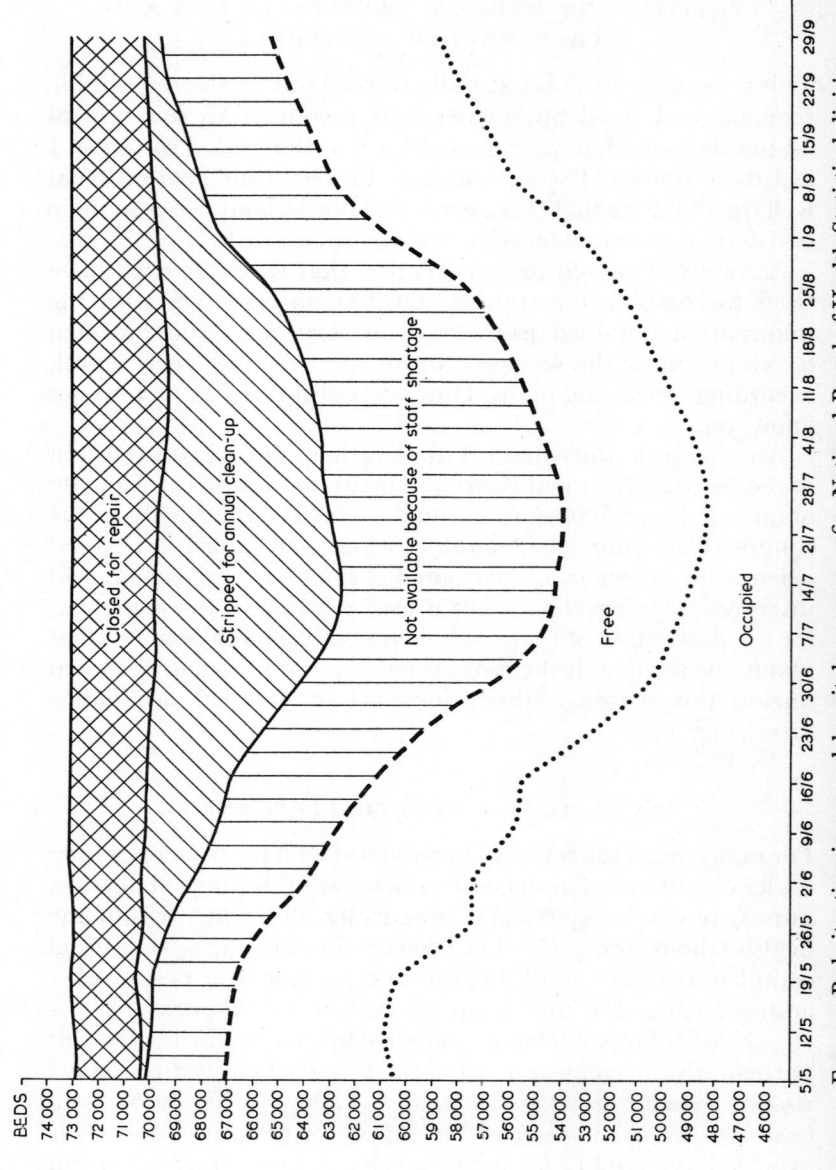

FIG. 14. Bed situation in general hospitals summer 1965. National Board of Health Statistical division.

geographical areas. This is important for the planning of educational programmes. The Medical Defence Planning Division of the National Board of Health is using those registers for the mobilization plans of medical personnel in case of war.

Twice a year data are collected to illustrate the personnel situation inside the services by requiring information *on vacant posts*. The figures received are important for our training programmes which of course, have to cover these vacancies, in addition to the demand for personnel for future plans. To get a sound balance between the evolution of the health services and trained personnel available during the years to come is a real headache for the national health authorities in the present affluent society.

This situation has indicated an expansion of the capacity of all medical and dental schools, schools of nursing etc., and

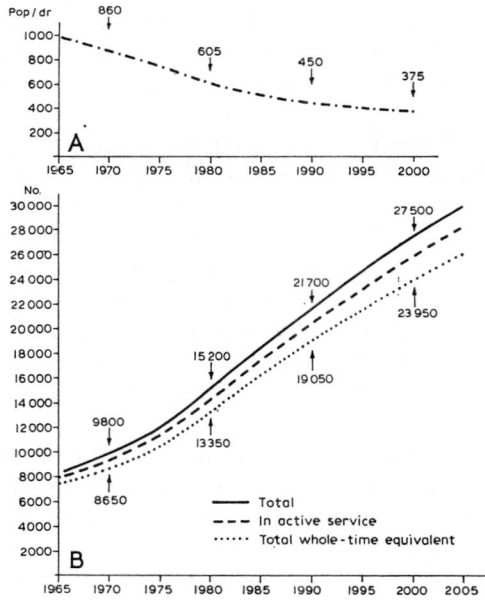

FIG. 15. A. Population/Doctor rate. B. Actual number of doctors 1965–1967. Expected number with present training programmes 1968—2005.

the establishment of new ones. In addition, several groups of new technical personnel, especially for laboratories, X-ray departments, operating theatres etc., have been trained. Other new careers are assistant nurses, and personnel for care of the aged, mainly domiciliary.

A continuous prognostic activity concerning all these groups of personnel is maintained. Fig. 15 is a diagram showing the availability of doctors during the coming years and illustrates how we work.

### MEDICAL ALERT STATISTICS

In medical alert statistics I include the statistical material originating from individual doctors and local health authorities' *reports on contagious diseases, accidents, poisonings, occupational health hazards,* etc., aiming at informing the central administration on environmental factors influencing the citizen's health. The *monitoring of adverse effects of drugs*—in Sweden not limited to abuse or dependence-producing drugs only—belongs to this group of data.

The *Cancer Register* (established 1958) also serves a similar purpose as does the *registration of stillbirths and abortions*.

For many years the maternity departments have reported *malformations observed in newborn babies*. This information was submitted to the national health administration yearly and was processed together with hospital morbidity figures, which at this time reached the central administration after the lapse of about one year following the end of each calendar year. The thalidomide disaster was in fact noticeable but the observation was made far too late

The new reporting system is a compulsory one and the reports have to be submitted monthly to the National Health Service's statistical department. In the following month a survey of the malformations diagnosed is provided and sent to the informants of *the malformation register* and several others. The standard deviation for every type of malformation has been calculated, so that when a malformation incidence surpasses the upper limit of the standard deviation it can immediately be recognised and a warning signal given. It is obvious that our present system of reporting would have identified the tragic thalidomide episode within five months of its beginning.

I have a feeling that this new tool will be of great value for the detection of prenatal damage of all kinds. The organization of the register will therefore be described in more detail.

The aim of statistics on congenital malformations and of the malformation register is to give current information month by month on the occurrence of newborn with malformations. It has only recently started; voluntary notification from certain obstetric departments began on 1 April 1964 and from 1 January 1965 was made compulsory. All maternity wards in the country which have a paediatric consultant must report. The total yearly number of deliveries in these wards is estimated at 70–75 000. The notifications have to be submitted to the National Board of Health.

The immediate responsibility for notification is laid upon the paediatrician. When he observes a malformation, he describes the abnormalities on a special record card which is partly transformed into a punch card. The name of the maternity service, birth date of the child and certain social data referring to the mother are also noted to make the tracing of the child possible, if this should be wanted later. The reports are submitted to the National Board of Health once monthly. The formal responsibility that the cards are delivered rests with the chief of the maternity department. In case of stillbirths or babies dead immediately after birth the chief of the delivery department is responsible also for editing the notification. Preparation and follow-up of the material submitted is done by medical specialists. All informants to the register are provided monthly with a survey of the malformations diagnosed. The notifications are to a certain degree of a confidential nature.

It is too early to give an opinion on the future development of these statistics. In the course of the pilot project on patient statistics from hospitals for physical diseases an attempt is being made to integrate the notification of malformations in newborn with the other information on the newborn which is part of that project.

Another instrument for the detection of dangerous environmental factors is the *Swedish Twin Register* founded in 1959 by Lars Friberg, Professor of Hygiene, Caroline Institute, Stockholm.

In the Institute of Hygiene of the Caroline Institute and the Department of General Hygiene of the National Institute of Public Health in Stockholm a register of twins was already being compiled in 1959 with a view to including all the twins of the same sex born in Sweden in the years 1886 to 1925 and still alive in 1959. The register lists some *12 000 pairs, 4 500 of them monozygotic and 7 500 dizygotic*. The classification of the pairs' zygosity was based on a questionnaire including a single question only, viz. 'Were you in childhood as like one another as two peas or were you of ordinary family likeness?' This proves to have a very high discriminating power when compared with a serological evaluation of 200 pairs.

This twin register as a matter of fact contains very useful information about constitutional factors and offers possibilities of extracting pure environmental factors in epidemiological studies. The register has been made use of in epidemiological studies of the health effects of tobacco smoking and air pollution. (Cederlöf and his colleagues). A co-twin control study on smoking in relation to coronary heart disease and lung function in twins (Lundman) has been made on a series of monozygotic twins discordant with respect to smoking. It seems that the excess morbidity and mortality from coronary heart disease reported in the large prospective study can be attributed to constitutional differences in smokers and non-smokers. Cederlöf also used the twin method in epidemiological studies on chronic disease. The twin approach offers the research workers a valuable tool and is a good supplement to other techniques. The work on planning that every national health administration certainly will find of a growing importance in years to come must be based on a very close co-operation with statisticians. In most countries a bureau of statistics is part of the central health administration. As I see it such statistical units with computer equipment have to be set up also at regional levels.

There must be a very close co-operation between programmes of health planning and of work in demography, vital statistics and statistics on social parameters, which as a rule are elaborated by an agency outside the health administration. This body badly needs the whole range of information to maintain an overall view of the health situation of the nation and its changes and for the rational planning of the services. As an intelligence agency the statistical division of a central health administration should always be prepared to collect information by employing fixed samples ready for use and by *ad hoc* studies, beside the massive routine collection of data.

The great opportunities of the modern electronic computers should be made more use of in medical research, in the management of all health services as well as in the practice of medicine. The appreciation of the potential of this new technology in medicine deserves a wider dispersal. Medical men and administrators should become more computer 'literate'. This is necessary in order to bring medical statistics to a thriving state.

## REFERENCES

CEDERLÖF, R. (1964) Tvillingregistret (The Twin Registry). *Nord Hyg. Tidskr.* **45**, 63.

CEDERLÖF, R., FRIBERG, L., JONSSON, E. and KAIJ, L. (1965) Morbidity among Monozygotic Twins. *Arch. of Environmental Health* **10**, 346.

CEDERLÖF, R. (1966) The Twin Method in Epidemiological Studies on Chronic Disease *Thesis* (Karolinska Institute), Stockholm: Esselte.

ENGEL, A. (1958) 'The Role of Hospital Statistics in Health Planning' in *Conference on Hospital Statistics and their Application in Health Administration*. Copenhagen: EURO, World Health Organization.

KÄLLEN, B. and WIKBERG, J. (1966) Erfarenheter av kontinuerlig registrering av missbildningar (Experiences of continuous Registration of Malformations). *Läkartidningen* **63**, 1941.

LINDHARDT (1960) *Sygdomsundersøgelsen i Danmark 1951–1954*. Copenhagen: Munksgaard.

LUNDMAN, T. (1966) Smoking in relation to coronary heart disease and lung function in twins *Acta Medica Scand.*, Suppl. 455, 16.

SJÖSTRÖM, Å. (1963) The continuous population sample—a source of statistical information in health administration. WHO Working group. Copenhagen: Euro—215 (3)/2.

SJÖSTRÖM, Å. (1963) Det svenska cancerregistret (Swedish Cancer registry) *Statistical Rev.* **1**, 42 (English Summary).

REPORTS:

*The Cancer Registry* (Annual Report) Cancer incidence in Sweden 1958–63. Stockholm: Kungl. Medicinalstyrelsen (National Board of Health).

*S.O.U. (Swedish Government Official Reports)* 1967, **25** and **41**. (1967) Government Commission on the Problem of Narcotic Addiction. Stockholm: Socialdepartementet (Ministry for Social Affairs).

*S.O.U. (Swedish Government Official Reports)* 1965, **49**. Government Commission on the National Administration of Health and Welfare Stockholm: Socialdepartementet (Ministry for Social Affairs). Annex 14.2.2.2. *Sjöström, Å.* The Statistical Department of the National Board of Health. English translation available through the Author. Address: Medicinalstyrelsen, Fack Stockholm 3.

*S.O.U. (Swedish Government Official Reports)* 1966, **28**. Government commission on provision of drugs by health insurance. Stockholm: Socialdepartementet (Ministry for Social Affairs). Excerpta:

Smedby, B. Receptundersökningen 1963 (The prescription investigation 1963).

Swarén, U. Läkemedelsreformen och läkemedelskonsumtionen 1965 (Health insurance legislation in respect of drugs and its effect on drug consumption 1965).

# 3
## MASS SCREENING FOR ASYMPTOMATIC DISEASE AS A PUBLIC HEALTH MEASURE

IN THIS lecture on mass screening for asymptomatic disease it is my intention to approach the subject as a public health measure and try to evaluate its importance in relation to the planning of the health services more specifically.

It is beyond my purpose to give a review of the history of modern medicine in its search for ways and means to detect disease at an early state. What I am going to describe and comment upon is mainly a mass screening programme that has recently been carried out in Sweden. The study has not yet been completed and several details remain to be analysed.

The term 'mass screening' indicates the screening of whole population groups where in principle no selection is made. The main purpose of this procedure is to sort out individuals with asymptomatic or unrecognized disease. By the term 'asymptomatic disease' I mean a disease without symptoms but in which signs can be demonstrated. This condition is however in practice more or less a fiction, even if every disease is likely to pass through such a phase. The intention is not primarily to arrive at a diagnosis. The main object is to detect suspected illness among apparently healthy persons and bring them under closer medical examination.

We are looking for ways and means of saving the time of skilled personnel (doctors and nurses) of whom Sweden has a shortage like many other countries. A sorting out procedure of those in real need of medical attention could be expected to ease the burden of these groups of personnel. Screening tests could be carried out by less trained personnel and should be automated as far as possible. Electronic data processing has made it feasible to collect and compile huge amounts of information for statistical purposes at reasonable cost and with less personnel than earlier.

The value of a screening depends on its validity in catching the pathological cases. The net used must have a fine enough mesh so that only very rarely can disease of any significance escape. This is extremely important and is the principal criterion of a good screening method. Nothing is more dangerous for the individual and more detrimental to the philosophy of mass screening and its application than to give an impression of false security to a person who has passed the screening tests without any remarks being made.

Mass screening can either be aimed at detecting disease in general and is then a multiphasic (multiple) screening, combining a number of tests, or it can be selective in respect of a population, an organ or a disease.

Selection can mean screening within specific population groups like high-risk groups in a dangerous occupation, children, cancer detection in age-groups at risk and so on. Screening can also be selective in searching for one or more specific diseases within a whole population, for instance for tuberculosis of the lung, diabetes, phenylketonuria (Fölling's disease).

TABLE 5. Conditions for which the Commission on Chronic Illness considered screening tests are now applicable. From *Chronic Illness in the United States*, vol. 1, *Prevention of Chronic Illness* (1957); Commission on Chronic Illness, Harvard University Press, Cambridge, Mass.

1. Pulmonary tuberculosis
2. Visual defects, including chronic glaucoma
3. Hearing defects
4. Syphilis
5. Diabetes mellitus
6. Cancer of skin, mouth, rectum, breast and cervix
7. Hypertensive disease
8. Ischaemic heart disease

Selective screening is much easier to handle, it has at least partly passed the experimental stage and is fully accepted by the medical profession. Already in 1957 the commission on chronic illness in U.S. published a list of conditions where they considered screening tests to be applicable (Table 5).

Later (1965), Dr Wilson, Ministry of Health, London,

added some further conditions which are detectable by rapid physical examination and also stressed the importance of asymptomatic bacteriuria.

The Kaiser Permanente Organization in U.S.A. provides to subscribers comprehensive prepaid medical care on an insurance basis. Their programme includes health surveillance to subscribers through the use of periodic health examinations.

Traditionally in an annual health check-up the physician conducts a regular examination (medical history, physical exploration) and then arranges a series of X-rays, laboratory tests etc. In the Kaiser Programme the patient first undergoes a battery of tests and procedures conducted in a highly automated laboratory with computer equipment (a psychological questionnaire is also included). The computer indicates if the results of certain tests have fallen outside normal limits and if further tests or special advice are needed. The physician receives a summary report when the patient comes for his first consultation. He directs further history-taking and examination by this information.

The centre is able to provide its examination at a cost of around £10.

The Kaiser Programme includes more conditions which may justify case-finding through screening procedures than those mentioned earlier.

In my country the scepticism against health control of a more general character still prevails in the medical profession. The attitude towards selective surveillance has on the other hand been mostly a positive one. I personally shared this opinion for a long time, strongly feeling the lack of suitable screening tests applicable to large unselected population groups and really useful in catching diseases of importance to the patient and to society e.g. cancer and cardiovascular diseases. To the well-known argument that screening is less valuable for diseases for which there exists no accepted treatment I was never very sensitive. I do not think it would do a man great harm to get his diagnosis a little earlier and a disease incurable today might be curable tomorrow. Neither have I been prepared to accept the obstacles of cost or non-existent facilities for the further diagnosis and treatment of detected cases.

In Sweden general mass photofluorography started in the

beginning of 1940 as part of the TB campaign. From 1946 on the whole population of the country was, by an Act of Parliament, recommended to be investigated with state financial support every fifth year. The contribution of this screening to the TB eradication programme has been very far-reaching. The reduction of the incidence of TB of the lungs has aroused an increasing interest in other pathological findings of the miniature X-ray picture of the chest, such as cancer of the lung and sarcoidosis. The smooth and effective organization of mass photofluorography made it natural to add other screening tests like analysis for the presence of sugar and albumin in the urine and a blood pressure record. Such studies have actually been done for several years in many counties of Sweden. My personal opinion was that sooner or later photofluorography ought to be incorporated into a sophisticated programme of periodic general health control of the population.

My mind was thus well prepared when I first heard of the development studies by the brothers Gunnar and Ingmar Jungner on chemical health screening. After consulting some of the scientific advisors, the National Board of Health in 1961 proposed to the Government that a health screening project covering 100 000 people should be carried out as an experiment, in association with mass photofluorography in the county of Värmland (Fig. 16). The field project was completed in 1964. However, I can only comment on some preliminary results and impressions, because the vast documentation collected has not yet been fully analysed.

The area for health screening was fairly distant, about 200 miles, from the National Board of Health, as well as from the Jungner laboratory. Many problems dependent on long distances had to be solved in a way that did not burden the ordinary health services and, especially, did not overload the hospitals. The following organization was used. I am here, with only small changes, following the description given by G. Jungner at the Colloqium held at Magdalen College, Oxford, in 1965 arranged by the Office of Health Economics.

A mobile field group for sample-taking and photofluorography etc. was organized; it moved from place to place, and could deal with 300 samples a day. The group changed location now and then, and was always in communication with a nearby hospital. The chemical analyses were done at a special laboratory for automation analysis in Stockholm with a capacity of 600–800 samples in 24 hours. At the National Board of Health, a group of experts (clinicians and statisticians) was formed with an office in Stockholm. The group was responsible for running the project. The medical follow-up of patients with positive findings was done at a medical station (a health centre).

All inhabitants from 25 years of age were offered the health screening. As a rule, health screening started by answering a questionnaire which contained only a few questions. At examination by the field group, height and weight were recorded, and also the time of taking the sample and of the last meal. The blood pressure was measured in a sitting position, because that was more convenient, although we are well aware that it can be criticized.

We know from experience, that it is very important to get the technique of blood-pressure taking correct. The sphygmomanometers were standardized against the mercury manometer every day; this was found to be absolutely necessary. This almost 'flying' blood-pressure measure has actually turned out to be reasonably accurate.

By experience, it became clear that blood pressure should be taken before a blood sample. It is always a question of which procedure upsets the patient most. If the patient expects a blood sample to be taken—nobody really likes it—the blood pressure should be taken before, not afterwards. We have tried both ways and have found that this is best. This was a voluntary investigation, of course, and we had a feeling that many persons would not like this new technique, but we were completely mistaken. We had a high percentage of attendances and almost all agreed to the blood sample being taken.

Each individual brought his urine sample to the medical station. As you will realize this is not a very safe technique, but for practical reasons we had to do it in this way. To take fresh urine specimens on such a large scale at the station is not practical. We had fairly good experience, and we have given quite a lot of information about ways to collect urine samples as correctly as possible. The urine specimen was analysed for the presence of sugar and protein by Clinistix and Albustix, respectively.

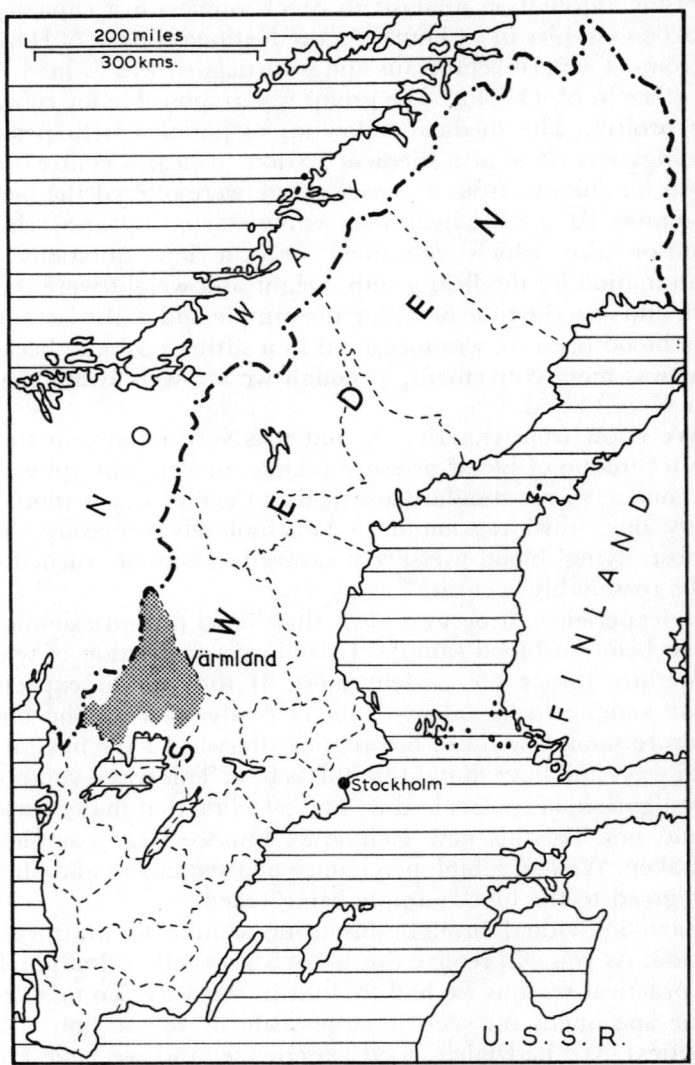

FIG. 16. Field area of the Värmland screening trial. Dotted lines mark the borders of the counties.

A blood sample was taken, and divided into a heparinized tube for determination of haemoglobin and haematocrit, and a tube for preparation of serum. When taking blood samples on a large scale, it is preferable to send them in chilled boxes to the laboratory, and this we did.

During the years 1962–4 invitations were sent to 116 638 persons over the age of 25, living in a population area of the county of Värmland representative from the socio-economic point of view of this county and of a typical province in central Sweden. Of those invited 74 per cent appeared for examination, together with about 2000 arriving uninvited—mostly workers of public or private enterprises being temporary residents of the area.

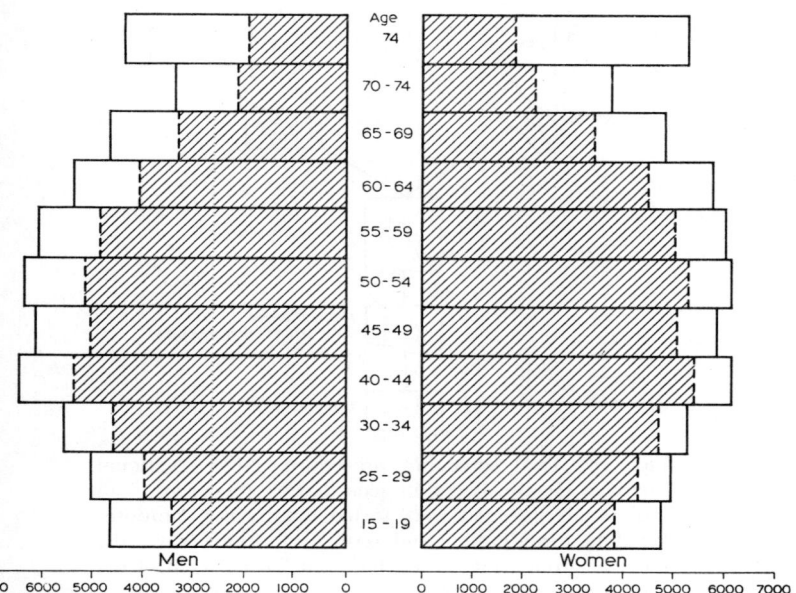

FIG. 17. Participation by age-group. The number of individuals invited was 116 638; of these 88 959 attended for examination (shaded area).

The number of those examined was 88 959. They were distributed by age and sex as can be seen from the above figure, which hardly needs any comment. Perhaps it should be noted that participation decreased in the highest age-groups, as would be expected.

The procedure of the Värmland trial is shown by the scheme below. It illustrates how the observations collected in the field arrive along two paths at the computer, where sorting is accomplished according to the programme given to the machine. The computer is thus doing medical selection—more or less a doctor's job.

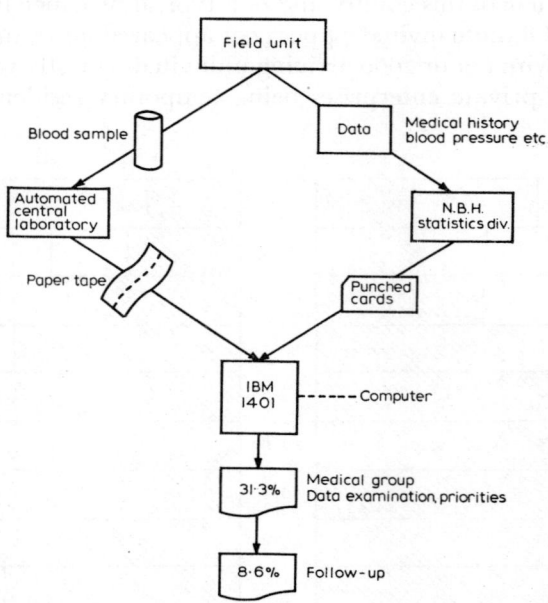

FIG. 18. Trial screening procedure. NBH = National Board of Health. It can be seen that 31·3 per cent of all individuals screened were sorted out by the computer for data examination and setting of priorities by the medical group. The group took out 8·6 per cent of the total number of screened persons for follow-up.

After many discussions, the National Board of Health finally decided that chemical health screening should comprise the following analyses: haemoglobin and haematocrit; serum-iron to detect iron deficiency states; creatinine as a renal function test; two enzyme tests: the transaminases, GOT and GPT, for liver damage; thymol turbidity, as well as the zinc sulphate test for gammaglobulin content; beta-lipoprotein and cholesterol and, finally, protein-bound hexoses and sialic acid to detect non-specific inflammatory states. The tests were selected in such a way that they partly overlapped, thus giving a higher significance.

TABLE 6. The complete screening programme.

| | |
|---|---|
| Medical history | Haemoglobin |
| Height | Haematocrit |
| Weight | Serum-Fe |
| Blood pressure | Creatinine |
| ⁄protein | GOT[1] |
| Urine | GPT[2] |
| ⧵sugar | Thymol |
| Photofluorography (chest) | Zinc sulphate |
| | Protein-bound hexose |
| | Sialic acid |
| | Beta-lipoprotein |
| | Cholesterol |

The programme operated by the computer produced information on very clear pathological parameters only. I shall come back later on to the question whether important diseases have been neglected through this procedure.

All positive findings of the screening referring to 31·3 per cent of all participants were scrutinized by the central group of clinicians, and the patients were grouped into six priority categories. The *priority standards* can be studied from *Appendix 1*, p. 65, which also gives information about the computer programme. Categories 1 to 3 consisted of patients where indications for a follow-up examination by a doctor were considered to be evident or even urgent. Patients who had already informed the screening patrol that they were under a doctor's care were as a rule thought to be satisfactorily taken care of and were therefore not followed up. It was also not feasible, for psychological reasons, to avoid sending patients already under treatment back to their own doctors.

As regards the follow-ups a weak point must be confessed

[1] Glutamic oxalacetic transaminase
[2] Glutamic pyruvic transaminase

immediately. The ideal would of course have been to have *one* instead of four highly qualified physicians permanently appointed for the whole period of this pilot study, making all the examinations and also participating in the final compilation of the results. Despite our efforts this was impossible and we greatly regret it. We were actually not able to recruit doctors for the follow-ups for more than a limited period of time.

Category 4 included cases where the blood chemistry findings were such as to indicate a repeated chemical analysis.

Category 5 contained controls of the urinary findings only.

The remaining category (O) consisted of persons, whose data were deemed to be of little significance and therefore did not indicate a follow-up but it also included all those who were for the time being under medical care. The wisdom of this last decision and of having a group of clinicians making priorities might be doubted, but as I said previously we could not do otherwise at that time. It should also be kept in mind that what we aimed at, in principle, was a screening for asymptomatic disease.

Individual regular medical examination was thus limited to a small group (8·6 per cent) of all screened people. A very strong selection was thus achieved. All diagnoses which were established refer to this group.

It should be observed that the Värmland investigation speaks of priorities (for further examinations) as a result of the screening procedure and of diagnoses after the follow-up only.

The photofluorography part of the Värmland trial has been reported on separately by Dr Bauer.[1] A long experience of this method is available and has been carefully analysed. Its reliability can be regarded as well established, especially since a vertical exposure was added to the usual frontal one. The results of the photofluorography can therefore be used for checking the validity of the chemical test battery in detecting diseases of the lung.

The idea is of course, that the two methods shall complement each other and be looked upon as a methodological entity.

It was never our intention to underestimate the individual

---

[1] Not yet published. In the following the expression 'health screening' means the Värmland trial exclusive of the photofluorographic examination.

physical examination and the painstaking medical history. On the contrary! We planned to find out if it was possible, and valuable, to screen out from a population those patients who needed a closer examination by reason of unrecognized diseases. This was done as a two step procedure—field-screening with automated data processing of the results, and analysis by a medical group of these results.

The group sorted out for the follow-up, 7620 patients, of whom 5539 had one or more diagnoses.

TABLE 7. Follow-up results of 7620 patients of a total of 88 959 screened.

|  | Male | | Female | | Total | |
|---|---|---|---|---|---|---|
|  | No. | % | No. | % | No. | % |
| Patients with diagnosis | 2179 | 64·1 | 3360 | 79·6 | 5539 | 72·7 |
| Patients without diagnosis | 1221 | 35·9 | 860 | 20·4 | 2081 | 27·3 |
| Total | 3400 | 100·0 | 4220 | 100·0 | 7620 | 100·0 |

TABLE 8. Of 5539 patients with one or more diagnoses, 3457 were considered in need of medical care or supervision.

|  | No. | Percentage of cases followed-up | Percentage of population screened |
|---|---|---|---|
| Patients admitted to hospitals | | | |
| Male | 195 | 5·7 | 0·4 |
| Female | 223 | 5·3 | 0·5 |
| Total | 418 | 5·5 | 0·5 |
| Referred to ambulatory care | | | |
| Male | 1011 | 29·7 | 2·3 |
| Female | 2028 | 48·1 | 4·5 |
| Total | 3039 | 39·9 | 3·4 |

Many administrators and doctors were afraid that the project would become a heavy burden for the hospitals of Värmland. This was, however, not the case. Of the total of those examined only 0·5 per cent were admitted to hospitals. The number of patients needing an ambulatory after-examination was also low (3·4 per cent of all those examined). This depended on the fact that as mentioned earlier a follow-up of patients already under a doctor's care was considered unnecessary.

Between the screening and the follow-up the interval of time varied greatly, partly because of the difficulty of recruiting doctors for the follow-up. On average the interval was 3 months. During the course of such a long period much might have happened to the patient.

TABLE 9. Diagnoses made by follow-up of 7620 individuals.

|  | Diag-noses | Indicated by the health screening | | Indicated previously unknown | | Non-indicated by the health screening | | Non-indicated previously unknown | |
|---|---|---|---|---|---|---|---|---|---|
|  |  | No. | % | No. | % | No. | % | No. | % |
| Male | 2639 | 1954 | 74·0 | 1193 | 61·1 | 685 | 26·0 | 367 | 53·6 |
| Female | 4165 | 3126 | 75·1 | 1821 | 58·3 | 1039 | 24·9 | 448 | 43·1 |
| Total | 6804 | 5080 | 74·7 | 3014 | 59·1 | 1724 | 25·3 | 815 | 47·3 |

Table 9, giving the diagnoses made at the follow-up of 7620 individuals, shows that 74·7 per cent of the 6804 diagnoses were indicated by the screening and that 59·1 per cent of them were previously unknown. In 25·3 per cent the diagnosis had not been indicated by the screening. Of these 45·9 per cent were unknown. It is not easy to evaluate these results. I would say they are not without promise.

The 791 *diagnoses* established by the follow-up but *not indicated* by the screening occurred mainly in Groups III, IV, VII and X of the WHO Classification of Diseases, Injuries and Causes of Death, as can be seen from Appendix 2, pp. 66–7.

*Group* III: Allergic, Endocrine, Metabolic, and Nutritional Diseases: Goitre (42 cases), diabetes (45), lipoidoses (40) and other metabolic diseases (19).

With exception of the findings of goitre the conditions seem very appropriate for chemical screening.

*Group* IV: Diseases of the Blood and Blood-forming Organs: Anaemia caused by bleeding (3), iron deficiency (39) and anaemia not specified (17).

*Group* VII: Diseases of the Circulatory System: in this group several cases of cardiosclerosis (23) and functional heart disorders (15) appear as well as peripheral arteriosclerosis (22). More unexpected, even when the variability of the blood pressure is considered, are the cases of hypertension with or without cardiac disease (159) as the blood pressure was actually taken at the screening.

*Group* x: Diseases of the Genito-urinary System: Hyperplasia of prostate (36). These were not unexpected.

Several of the pathological conditions mentioned above are likely to be recognized by the screening method. Of course, the yield would have been higher if we had used less rigorous limits for the different test values. The observations also indicate the desirability of E.C.G. and tests for bacteriuria in future trials.

It is not yet possible to present in a general review how the different groups of diseases, and still less the particular disease, have been sorted out and by which tests of the chemical test battery.

*The four diagnostic groups found most frequently* are presented in Table 10, and I would like to make a few comments on the figures.

TABLE 10. The four most frequently indicated diagnoses.

| Diagnosis (Classif. No.) | Total | | Indicated by the health screening | | Previously unknown | | Prevalence in the screened population (per thousand) |
|---|---|---|---|---|---|---|---|
| | No. | % | No. | % | No. | % | |
| Diabetes (260) | 505 | 100·0 | 417 | 82·6 | 305 | 60·4 | 5·7 |
| Hypercholesterolemia (289.0) | 456 | 100·0 | 414 | 90·6 | 394 | 86·4 | 5·1 |
| Hypochromic anaemias (291) | 1320 | 100·0 | 1270 | 96·2 | 897 | 68·0 | 14·8 |
| Hypertension (440-47) | 1919 | 100·0 | 1550 | 80·8 | 788 | 41·1 | 21·6 |

As can be seen, the four listed diagnoses have been indicated by the health screening at rather high percentages. As regards hypertension a higher frequency could have been expected but the computer was programmed to sort out blood pressure values over 115 diastolic in men and 120 in women. A blood-sugar test on an empty stomach or up to two hours after a glucose load, as in the Bedford investigation, would certainly have increased the number of pathological findings.

Without random control material it is not feasible to evaluate these results fully. This control is unfortunately lacking but an attempt to evaluate the sorting out effect in respect to need of hospital care has, however, been made.

All *persons* (155) *with negative screening results from 7 subsequent investigation days were called upon for a meticulous follow-up 3 to 4 months afterwards.* Of these, 121 attended and were examined. The remaining 34 were approached on the telephone and 28 reported that they enjoyed perfect health. Through the health insurance, information was obtained on the other six. One was ill with digestive troubles for 6 weeks the remaining five were not reported as being ill.

Observed diagnoses were as follows:

(1) Important and indicating hospital care immediately: three cases all with tumours (cancer of the pancreas, cancer recti and hypophyseal tumour).

(2) Important and in need of ambulatory medical care: One case of asthma. (The doctor noted that it could be a collagenous disease.)

(3) Less important: Medical advice and possibly prescription indicated in certain cases but no other measures: 47 cases.

(4) Unimportant: 70 persons.

The number of cases where hospital care was indicated represented 2·5 per cent of this control-group if it comprises the examined cases only. If this figure is compared with the corresponding one from the follow-up, 5·5 per cent, it seems likely, but not significantly so, that a screening function has been achieved. The control group was thus too small to give reliable information even on the question for which it was originally chosen.

The screening procedure was not aiming specifically at detecting cancer, but of course the *malignant tumours* must for many reasons be regarded as a main target in every health screening, not least because cancer tends to remain silent for a long period and because of its high incidence and serious prognosis. It is therefore of great interest to study how effective the Värmland investigation was in this respect.

It is compulsory for the doctor responsible for the treatment to report all cases of malignant tumours to the Swedish cancer register. All biopsies and autopsies at which cancer has been observed have also to be reported. This gives an opportunity to follow up the cancer diagnoses indicated by the screening and also to study how many cases pass unrecognized.

If the period of observation is fixed at 12 months after the screening (that is, if all cases which are considered are reported to the cancer register within one year after the screening) 64 cases were indicated by the chemical tests out of 221 reported to the registry in this population, that is 29 per cent.

If the period of observation is 6 months, the corresponding figures are 33 of 98, which is 34 per cent. This is hardly a satisfactory result.

In the following table the diagnoses of *active pulmonary diseases* are shown as they have been established by the follow-up of the mass-photofluorography under the auspices of the TB

TABLE 11. Major pulmonary diagnoses from photofluorography compared with the results of the screening trial.

| Diagnosis (central TB dispensary) | No. | Indicated by the health screening | | Non-indicated by the health screening | |
|---|---|---|---|---|---|
| | | No. | % | No. | % |
| Active pulmonary TB | 62 | 24 | 38·7 | 38 | 61·3 |
| Pneumonia | 20 | 7 | 35·0 | 13 | 65·0 |
| Malignant tumour | 16 | 8 | 50·0 | 8 | 50·0 |
| Sarcoidosis | 72 | 18 | 25·0 | 54 | 75·0 |
| Total | 170 | 57 | 33·5 | 113 | 66·5 |

central station of Värmland. The cases are broken down into two groups, indicated and non-indicated by the screening procedure previously described. It is remarkable that the chemical and clinical tests indicated only 38·7 per cent of the cases of active TB. Less unexpected is the fact that not more than

50 per cent of the malignant tumours of the lung and 18 per cent of sarcoidosis cases were revealed. Between the miniature X-ray screening and the follow-up there was an interval of 1 to 2 months.

SUMMARY

IT WAS SHOWN that the fieldproject could be carried out by a small group of six including one X-ray technician and one nurse but no doctor. They successfully managed the screening procedure in a large population. This deserves to be noted.

Many problems dependent on long distances were solved, e.g. as regards the taking and the transport of the samples in chilled boxes. All these experiences will be of great practical value for similar trials in the future.

Thanks to the health authorities and the medical profession of Värmland cases observed to be in need of immediate care were taken care of without delay—a fact that should be gratefully acknowledged.

It is also worth mentioning that *the cost* of the Värmland trial was comparatively low, amounting to *roughly £3 per person examined*. There are good reasons to believe that in the future this cost can be considerably reduced.

The laboratory was processing its data very speedily and without any interruptions of function.

As can be understood from the planning of the Värmland trial, its main purpose was to study the validity of the chemical test-battery as a new element in a larger health screening project. The value of photofluorography, the test for the presence of protein and sugar in the urine, blood pressure measure etc., are elements previously studied separately by many others, in contradistinction to the multiple chemical screening. Some of the components of the test-battery like haemoglobin, haematocrit and serum iron give direct information of immediate value as regards the medical case of the individual examined. About the same can be said of cholesterol. Here the results involve a risk of confusing both the doctor and his patient, especially as a slightly increased cholesterol-value is not easily evaluated and consequent treatment is often doubtful.

The extent to which the other separate chemical tests have contributed to indicate asymptomatic disease or recognise pathology is still a subject to be analysed, as is the correlation between the different tests.

It is, however, clear that chemical screening has been able to sort out diseases in need of hospital care to a certain, but not well defined, extent.

Of all indicated diagnoses nearly 60 per cent were previously unknown.

If the Värmland trial has exercised a screening function—was it a satisfactory one from the medical point of view? A reminder—it was a pilot study planned as such and meant to evaluate chemical screening separately. In a final form the chemical screening, revised according to experiences of the Värmland trial, has to be co-ordinated with medical history taking, physical examination, radiography and probably with E.C.G. and a test for bacteriuria.

To the question I have posed my answer is *not yet*. A higher precision in sorting out pathological conditions especially those belonging to the chronic, socially important diseases like malignant tumours and cardiovascular diseases is required. Multiple health screening aiming at early diagnosis of chronic diseases must be regarded as still on the experimental level.

As a public health man and a former clinician I feel, nevertheless, that it is a strategy we have to follow up.

Our service-rendering welfare state has a mounting demand for medical services not least of a preventive nature—health education and health control are especially popular. It is the medical profession which has for decades taught the public the importance of early diagnosis and health check-ups. We have a responsibility here. Before a multiple screening method is presented to the public as a general health control practice, a very high reliability must be guaranteed. This has not yet been reached.

A mass screening method with the purpose of detecting pathology in general within a population could, as I see it, become a useful tool in the hands of the public health authorities and be combined with tests for selected information on specific health matters. Applied as an *ad hoc* study it could already be of great value in providing a better knowledge of the pattern of disease in relation to demography and geography. Morbidity epidemiology in general would certainly profit from undertakings of this kind. How tempting it would be just now to add the determination of folic acid to the test battery!

Mass health screening will no doubt largely contribute in the future to elucidating the natural history of many diseases, for instance bacteriurias and pyelonephritis. A forthcoming publication based on the Värmland trial will offer clinical pathology valuable information on normal values and ranges of all the tests used, grouped by age and sex and perhaps geographical distribution. The lack of such information has been expressed many times (cf. Richterich's manual).

An early diagnosis will always be desirable and mass examination for the finding of early cases of disease must therefore continue. This means that new and better diagnostic methods, chemical or others, applicable on a mass scale must be invented. Selective screening methods, however, will certainly dominate the practice of medicine for some years to come.

## APPENDIX 1

Priority standards to guide the medical group.

| | | | Lowest priority group |
|---|---|---|---|
| 1 *Beta-lipoprotein* | $\geq$17 units (in combination with other findings*) | | 3 |
| 2 *Cholesterol* | | | |
| Increased value | $\geq$400 mg–% | | 3 |
| Subnormal value | $\leq$170 mg–% | | 3 |
| 3–4 *Transaminase* | | | |
| GOT: | 41– 60 units (comb.) | | 3 |
| | 61–100 ,, | | 3 |
| | $\geq$100 ,, | | 2 |
| GPT: | 41– 60 ,, | | 4 |
| | 61–100 ,, | | 3 |
| | $\geq$100 ,, | | 2 |
| 5 *Thymol* | $\geq$8 units (comb.) | | 3 |
| 6 *Creatinine* | 1·8–2·2 mg–% | | 4 |
| | $\geq$2·3 mg–% | | 3 |
| | $\geq$2·8 mg–% | | 2 |
| 7–8 *Hexose-Sialic Acid* | | | |
| (a) no infection | 140–147 Hex, 80–85 Sia (if both pos. and age > 40 years) | | 4 |
| | $\geq$148 Hex $\geq$86 Sia | | 3 |
| (b) infection | 148–154 Hex, 86-88 Sia | | 4 |
| | $\geq$155 Hex 89 Sia | | 3 |
| 9 *Zinc Sulphate* | $\geq$ 13 units | | 3 |
| | $\leq$ 3 ,, | | 3 |
| 10 *Haemoglobin* | | | |
| men | $\leq$7·0 g–% | women $\leq$ 7·0 g–% | 1 |
| | 7·1– 9·5 g–% | 7·1– 9·5 g–% | 2 |
| | 9·6–11·0 g–% | 9·6–10·5 g–% | 3 |
| 11 *Haematocrit* | | | |
| men | $\leq$36% | women $\leq$35% | 3 |
| 12 *Serum Iron* | | 0–39 µg–% (no infection) | 3 |
| | | 40–50 µg–% (comb., no infection) | 3 |
| *Blood Pressure* | | | |
| men | $\geq$210/115 | women $\geq$220/120 | 3 |
| | $\geq$230/130 | $\geq$230/130 | 2 |

* The abbreviation 'comb.' is used in the following.

# APPENDIX 2
## DIAGNOSES MADE AT FOLLOW-UP

| Diagnostic group | | Grand total | Thereof | | | | |
|---|---|---|---|---|---|---|---|
| | | | indicated by the health screening | | | non-indicated by the health screening | |
| | | | total | previously | | total | previously |
| | | | | un-known | known | | un-known known |

| Diagnostic group | | Grand total | indicated total | indicated previously un-known | indicated previously known | non-indicated total | non-indicated previously un-known | non-indicated previously known |
|---|---|---|---|---|---|---|---|---|
| I Infective and parasitic diseases | M | 19 | 13 | 4 | 9 | 6 | 1 | 5 |
| | F | 19 | 10 | 3 | 7 | 9 | 2 | 7 |
| | M+F | 38 | 23 | 7 | 16 | 15 | 3 | 12 |
| II Neoplasms | M | 56 | 42 | 22 | 20 | 14 | 11 | 3 |
| | F | 67 | 39 | 32 | 7 | 28 | 27 | 1 |
| | M+F | 123 | 81 | 54 | 27 | 42 | 38 | 4 |
| III Allergy, endocrine system, metabolic and nutritional diseases | M | 596 | 415 | 341 | 74 | 181 | 65 | 116 |
| | F | 895 | 487 | 390 | 97 | 408 | 111 | 297 |
| | M+F | 1491 | 902 | 731 | 171 | 589 | 176 | 413 |
| IV Diseases of the blood and bloodforming organs | M | 245 | 215 | 175 | 40 | 30 | 26 | 4 |
| | F | 1181 | 1137 | 781 | 356 | 44 | 35 | 9 |
| | M+F | 1426 | 1352 | 956 | 396 | 74 | 61 | 13 |
| V Mental diseases | M | 13 | 3 | – | 3 | 10 | – | 10 |
| | F | 10 | – | – | – | 10 | 6 | 4 |
| | M+F | 23 | 3 | – | 3 | 20 | 6 | 14 |
| VI Diseases of the nervous system | M | 12 | – | – | – | 12 | 4 | 8 |
| | F | 16 | 1 | – | 1 | 15 | 6 | 9 |
| | M+F | 28 | 1 | – | 1 | 27 | 10 | 17 |
| VII Circulatory diseases | M | 903 | 658 | 366 | 292 | 245 | 139 | 106 |
| | F | 1334 | 990 | 462 | 528 | 344 | 158 | 186 |
| | M+F | 2237 | 1648 | 828 | 820 | 589 | 297 | 292 |
| VIII Respiratory diseases | M | 138 | 111 | 13 | 98 | 27 | 18 | 9 |
| | F | 93 | 71 | 3 | 68 | 22 | 10 | 12 |
| | M+F | 231 | 182 | 16 | 166 | 49 | 28 | 21 |

FOR ASYMPTOMATIC DISEASE

| Diagnostic group | | Grand total | Thereof | | | | |
|---|---|---|---|---|---|---|---|
| | | | indicated by the health screening | | | non-indicated by the health screening | |
| | | | total | previously | | total | previously |
| | | | | un-known | known | | un-known | known |
| IX | Diseases of the digestive system M | 170 | 137 | 101 | 36 | 33 | 20 | 13 |
| | F | 80 | 53 | 27 | 26 | 27 | 14 | 13 |
| | M+F | 250 | 190 | 128 | 62 | 60 | 34 | 26 |
| X | Diseases of the genito-urinary system M | 209 | 140 | 64 | 76 | 69 | 47 | 22 |
| | F | 118 | 90 | 27 | 63 | 28 | 12 | 16 |
| | M+F | 327 | 230 | 91 | 139 | 97 | 59 | 38 |
| XI | Complications of pregnancy and the puerperium M | – | – | – | – | – | – | – |
| | F | 12 | 11 | 9 | 2 | 1 | – | 1 |
| XII | Diseases of the skin M | 12 | 3 | – | 3 | 9 | 3 | 6 |
| | F | 20 | 8 | 2 | 6 | 12 | 6 | 6 |
| | M+F | 32 | 11 | 2 | 9 | 21 | 9 | 12 |
| XIII | Diseases of the bones, joints, etc. M | 128 | 102 | 10 | 92 | 26 | 7 | 19 |
| | F | 160 | 120 | 8 | 112 | 40 | 6 | 34 |
| | M+F | 288 | 222 | 18 | 204 | 66 | 13 | 53 |
| XIV | Congenital malformations M | 3 | 2 | 1 | 1 | 1 | 1 | – |
| | F | 7 | 2 | 1 | 1 | 5 | 4 | 1 |
| | M+F | 10 | 4 | 2 | 2 | 6 | 5 | 1 |
| XVI | Senility and ill-defined conditions M | 134 | 113 | 91 | 22 | 21 | 17 | 4 |
| | F | 150 | 106 | 70 | 36 | 44 | 33 | 11 |
| | M+F | 284 | 219 | 161 | 58 | 65 | 50 | 15 |
| XVII | Accidents, poisoning and violence M | 1 | – | – | – | 1 | – | 1 |
| | F | 3 | 1 | – | 1 | 2 | 2 | – |
| | M+F | 4 | 1 | – | 1 | 3 | 2 | 1 |
| All diagnoses | M | 2639 | 1954 | 1188 | 766 | 685 | 359 | 326 |
| | F | 4165 | 3126 | 1815 | 1311 | 1039 | 432 | 607 |
| | M+F | 6804 | 5080 | 3003 | 2077 | 1724 | 791 | 933 |

## REFERENCES

BAUER, H. (1967) Personal communication (mass radiography) in the Värmland trial).

BJÖRNESJÖ, K-B. (1966) Kemiska mätbara förändringar i blodplasma som indikator på aktiv vävnadsprocess (Chemically measurable changes in blood plasma indicating active tissue process). *Läkartidningen* **63**, 2658.

BOLIN and COLL. (1966) Fakta från försöksverksamhet med utökad hälsokontroll (Observations from the Värmland screening trial). *Läkartidningen* **62**, 1231.

BRANTE, G., OLAFSSON, O., RIGNER, K. and SUNDELIN, G. (1966) Kliniskt-kemiska analysmetoder vid två pilotundersökningar i Eskilstuna (Clinical chemical analytic methods used in two pilot studies in the city of Eskilstuna). *Läkartidningen* **63**, 2602.

COLLEN, M. F. (1965) 'A multiphasic screening programme' in *Surveillance and early diagnosis in general practice*, edited by Teeling-Smith, London: Office of Health Economics.

HALLBERG, L. (1966) Anemi och hälsoundersökning (Anaemia and health screening) *Läkartidningen* **63**, 2669.

HAMBRAEUS, A., HENNING, C. and MÉLÉN, B. (1966) (A chemical method to diagnose urinary infections). *Läkartidningen* **62**, 1226.

JOSEPHSON, B. (1966) Möjligheten att avslöja njursjukdom vid folkhälsoundersökningar (The feasibility of detecting renal disease through mass health screening). *Läkartidningen* **63**, 2665.

JUNGNER, G. (1965) Chemical health screening in *Surveillance and early diagnosis in general practice*, edited by Teeling-Smith, London: Office of Health Economics.

JUNGNER, G. and JUNGNER, I. (1965) The Health Screening project in Värmland. Ibid.

JUNGNER, G. and JUNGNER, I. (1964) A pilot study on mass screening with application of a chemical test battery—The health screening project in Värmland. *Report of the 14th Session of the Committee for Europe of the WHO in Prague* (Stencile). Copenhagen: Euro.

JUNGNER, I. (1966) Erfarenheter från Värmlandsundersökningen (Experiences from the Värmland trial). *Läkartidningen* **63**, 2602.

LJUNG, O. (1966) Ett diskussionsinlägg om Värmlandsundersökningen (The Värmland trial, a debate statement). *Läkartidningen* **63**, 2675.

NORDEN, Ä. (1966) Hälsokontroll: En internists syn på uppläggning och metodval för riktad kontroll (An internist's view on ways and means of selected health control. *Läkartidningen* **63**, 2578.

SCHERSTEN, B. (1966) Värdering av screening metoder för diabetes (Evaluation of screening methods for diabetes). *Läkartidningen* **63**, 2659.

TIBBLIN, G. (1966) Allmän hälsoundersökning av män i Göteborg (General health control of men in the city of Gothenburg). *Läkartidningen* **63**, 2588.

WEGELIUS, C. (1967) The benefit of mass chest surveys for early detection of non-tuberculous findings. Unpublished. Personal communication.

WILSON, J. M. (1965) Some principles of early diagnosis and detection in *Surveillance and early diagnosis in general practice*, edited by Teeling-Smith. London: Office of Health Economics.

SJÖSTRÖM, Å. (1966) *Symposium sur l'Emploi des Ordinateurs électroniques dans les Statistiques sanitaires et la Recherche médicale*. Application du traitement electronique de l'information dans une étude épidémiologique. WHO Copenhagen: Euro –341/3

# 4
## THE SWEDISH REGIONALIZED HOSPITAL AND HEALTH SYSTEM

### DEVELOPMENT AT THE COUNTY LEVEL

1862 WAS a remarkable year in Swedish social and political history. In that year community self-government was instituted by new laws for the local communes and—most important— on the basis of the historical state-governed counties a new regional self-governing body was created—the county council. This was elected by the citizens of the county and empowered with the right to impose taxes. Among the duties of the county councils, as laid down by the new legislation, health care— until then entirely a state concern—was included. The responsibility for the care of the mentally ill and the district doctor organization stayed, however, with the state. Almost at once the administration of the hospital system became the most important task of the county councils and has so remained. Not less than about 85 per cent of their budgets are allocated to medical care. Environmental sanitation was never a responsibility of the county councils but of the local communes and in this respect no change is planned.

Immediately after being taken over by the county councils the Swedish hospital system entered into a development phase that has made our hospitals world famous. As I see it this happened because the responsibility for the evolution was placed with a self-governing, locally elected body which knew the needs and understood the psychology of the population. It was also most important that the county as a rule had an appropriate population-size and rather homogenous socioeconomic conditions.

The full consequences of the 1862 legislation was, however, only achieved one hundred years later during the 1960s, when the county councils successively were made legally responsible in principle for the whole sector of medical care.

At about the turn of the century all counties had one or more hospitals, as a rule without any specialized departments. In the large cities, however, specialization had already begun. During the nineteen twenties and thirties there emerged the so-called *central hospital of the county* with a steadily increasing number of specialties.

It gradually became a well established experience that a population of about 250 000, which is the average of a Swedish county today (range 60 000 to 400 000) is big enough as a base for the development of a modern specialized hospital. The central hospitals have up to 14–16 specialized departments of a reasonable capacity and several laboratory and other technical services. The recommended pattern was in the late 50s and still is as shown in Table 12.

TABLE 12. Clinical departments and other services recommended for central hospitals

| Central Hospital | |
|---|---|
| Departments with wards | Other services |
| Internal Medicine | Radiology |
| General Surgery | Clinical Physiology |
| Anaesthesics | Biochemistry |
| Paediatrics | Microbiology |
| Gynaecology and Obstetrics | Blood transfusion |
| E.N.T. | Pathological Anatomy |
| Ophthalmology | Dental clinic |
| Infectious diseases | M.C.H. centre |
| Pneumology | Child Guidance clinic |
| Orthopaedic Surgery | Family Planning Advisory centre |
| Psychiatry | Speech and Hearing centres |
| Child Psychiatry | |
| Long-term diseases | |
| Rehabilitation clinic and Physiotherapy | |
| Neurology[1] | |
| Dermatology[1] | |

During the last 15 years requirements for hospital beds have been intensively studied. Attempts have been made to estimate the number of beds in general and of different specialties in

[1] In larger counties only.

relation to population; so-called *bed quotas* (bed/population rates). As has already been pointed out these figures are highly dependent on the age-structure of the population. They must also vary with the prevalence of disease among the population in respect of the total pattern, as well as of the frequency of the individual diseases. Many other factors are also involved, e.g. social and economic. Health insurance schemes can thus have an effect in either raising the demand for hospital beds, as is the situation in Sweden with completely free hospital care and lesser benefits for ambulatory and domiciliary care, or bringing them down where consultations are favourably covered by insurance. The housing situation in certain areas may influence the tendency to hospitalization just as a strong family tradition may be effective in the opposite way especially in the case of old people, for example as in Israel.

The value of minimum standard rates for hospital beds '*bed quotas*' is—this must be frankly underlined—a limited one. If the figures are related to age-groups (consumer units)[1] they are more reliable as a base for hospital planning but there is still much criticism left. However, *if we take them with a pinch of salt they are in our experience indispensable in hospital planning as a crude guide.* I present below the Swedish figures used for hospital planning in the counties by the National Board of Health and by the special Commission on Hospital Planning and Equipment. They are entirely based on the experiences of the last 15 years' hospital planning and they have been revised from time to time. Prominent causes for revision have been the marked decrease of infectious diseases and increase of diseases related to old age.

Psychiatric beds are for the time being in a flux as to their numbers. The old-fashioned mental hospitals are being reorganized to take care of mainly chronic psychoses and geriatric cases. The number of psychiatric beds is slowly decreasing and acute psychiatry more and more shifting over to psychiatric departments in general hospitals as is indicated in Table 13.

Around the central hospital and its many specialized outpatient departments were grouped so-called 'normal' hospitals. When I worked out the regional hospital plan (1956–58) it was suggested that internal medicine, general surgery, radiology

[1] See page 11 (Table 1).

TABLE 13. Hospital beds in relation to population as recommended by the Swedish National Board of Health.

| General hospitals | Beds per 1,000 population | Mental hospitals and institutions | Beds per 1,000 population |
|---|---|---|---|
| Internal Medicine | 1·4–1·5 | Mental hospitals (under reorganization) | <3·6 |
| General Surgery | 1·3–1·4 | Mental nursing homes | 1·0 |
| Paediatrics | 0·3 | Mental Retardation | |
| Gynaecology | 0·3–0·4 | Special hospitals (multiple disability, low grades) | 0·3–0·4 |
| Obstetrics | 0·5 | Institutions for residential care, hostels | 2·0–3·0 |
| E.N.T. | 0·15–0·19 | | |
| Ophthalmology | 0·12 | Total | 6·9–8·0 |
| Infectious diseases | 0·2–0·3 | | |
| Pneumology | 0·4 | | |
| Urology | 0·2 | | |
| Orthopaedic Surgery | 0·3–0·4 | | |
| Psychiatry | 0·3 | | |
| Child Psychiatry | 0·1 | | |
| Long-term diseases[1] | 0·25 | | |
| (in nursing homes) | (3·75) | | |
| Total | 5·82–6·36 | | |

[1] As a rule calculated only on individuals aged 70 and over and suggested to be 55 per 1000 of the population = 4 per thousand of population at present.

and anaesthesiology be represented at the *'normal'* hospital. We now mostly call them *district hospitals*.

The success of the county hospital scheme which I have described has step by step convinced the politicians and the medical profession of the advantage of having the county councils responsible for all medical care including individual preventive measures.

The county councils in accordance with a parliamentary act of 1961 took over the district doctors and their centres. A better integration between medical care inside and outside the hospital will thereby be achieved. From January 1, 1967, the county councils became responsible for the administration of the mental hospitals run previously by the State. The State is thereafter responsible—apart from its overall planning, supervising and controlling functions as regards the whole health system—only for environmental sanitation and a few small branches of highly specialized institutional services (for the criminal psychopaths, the blind, and the deaf). The responsibility for environmental hygiene, however, is divided between the smallest administrative units (the communes) and the state.

Even if experience has shown that the counties have been capable of building up highly differentiated hospital facilities there it has been fully evident that they were not large enough to support such specialties as neurosurgery, thoracic surgery, radiotherapeutic cancer clinics, virology, etc.

In our country, as everywhere, all new branches of medicine first emerge at the teaching hospitals. Exceptions, however, exist, and there are a few examples of world-famous clinics for new and highly specialized disciplines established at municipal non-teaching hospitals around a professional man of high competence and strength of will.

### THE REGIONAL HOSPITAL PLAN

In 1956 I was appointed by the government as a one-man commission to study the need of resources for the most specialized hospital services and to advise on a suitable organization to provide this care on a nation-wide scale. Medical reasons are not the sole justification for a rational organization. Sound economy in the use of medical personnel and of available funds are important, too. Equipment and running costs are, as is well known, extremely high for those services requiring a concentration in units of a sufficient number of beds. Large units are furthermore indicated to secure a clientèle large enough for practical and scientific studies and for teaching purposes. It is an important task to balance the factors speaking in favour of high centralization against those indicating decentralization, e.g. an understandable wish of the public to have medical facilities within a convenient distance. In spite of excellent communications the last mentioned circumstance must be duly considered in a hospital plan for a country like Sweden so sparsely populated in its wide northern areas.

The terms of reference of my commission now required a higher organizational level for, let us call them, super-specialties.

I started by holding a series of hearings with representatives of the most specialized branches of medicine—by then to be found very irregularly distributed and mainly at teaching hospitals—asking their opinions on the need for hospital beds for their different specialties, the optimum size of departments, etc. By means of a questionnaire to the hospitals the present activity within the following branches was analysed: neurosurgery, thoracic surgery, plastic surgery, radiotherapy, neurology, dermatology, urology and child surgery. Waiting lists were also required.

The estimated standard figures arrived at were very close to those we are following today and which you find in Table 14.

The first three specialties of Table 14 have determined the size of the region because they deal with rare diseases. A strong centralization seems indispensable here for getting clinical units (wards) of an appropriate size for treatment for the training of specialists and for clinical research. The majority of cases belonging to neurology, dermatology or urology can and should be taken care of in departments of internal medicine and general surgery of county central hospitals, whereas the recommended regional unit should provide treatment for the most complicated cases. As regards child surgery the requirement for beds is high in the large cities, where all children with surgical diseases are expected to consult a child surgery department. In other areas it has been found most practical to leave it to the general surgeon to take care of the majority of children, representing as a rule emergency cases. Only those cases which need the experience and the technical skill of the child surgeon have to be sent to him.

TABLE 14. Bed/population rate for superspecialties.

| | Beds per 100000 population | |
|---|---|---|
| Plastic Surgery | 5.5 | |
| Thoracic Surgery | 4.6 | |
| Neurosurgery | 4.1 | |
| Radiotherapy (Cancer clinics) | 14 | (at least 1/4 for gynaecological cancer) |
| Neurology | 12–16 | (divided between regional and county levels) |
| Dermatology | 10–15 | (rural areas) |
| | 20–30 | (large cities) |
| Urology | 20 | (divided between regional and county levels) (2/3 male patients) |

| | Beds per 100000 children under 15 years of age | |
|---|---|---|
| Paediatric Surgery | 100 | (densely populated areas) |
| | 20 | (sparsely populated areas) |

From the above-mentioned calculations it was apparent that in accordance with experience from abroad (U.K., U.S.A. and France) about 1 million inhabitants would be necessary for setting up a hospital with the specialties we had in mind and with a sufficient number of beds to constitute a desirable clinical unit.

The next step was to *nominate* those among the large hospitals which seemed to become most suitable as *regional* hospitals. The five teaching hospitals (Caroline Hospital, Stockholm, University Hospital, Lund-Malmö, Sahlgrenska Hospital, Gothenburg; Academic Hospital, Uppsala; and Umeå in the northern part of the country) were the obvious choice from the beginning. In order to draw up the boundaries of the regions an expert in economic geography was asked to study the problem from the point of view of demographic and economic development as well as of transport. It was clear from the beginning that if possible a county should not be divided between two regions and that we had to prepare in the vast sparsely populated northern region for a smaller number of inhabitants than the ideal of one million.

The geographer, Prof. Godlund, has published his studies separately.[1] The reader interested in the details is referred to this paper. Here I shall only point out that these potential regional hospital sites were earmarked by me and analysed by Prof. Godlund from his special points of view, taking into consideration the population and transport situation in the year 1955 (the last available figures when the study was made) and its probable development up to 1970.

The commission recommended seven hospital regions to be organized, six at once and the seventh from 1970.

The counties were supposed to collaborate in the regionalization plan on a voluntary basis. The county in which the regional hospital is situated should run the regional hospital and the other counties should pay for the costs of the treatment of their patients, i.e. for running as well as investment costs.

Additional recommendations were that the co-operation between the counties should start with the following clinical branches: neurosurgery, neuromedicine, thoracic surgery, plastic surgery, urology, child surgery, radiotherapy, dermatology and rheumatology[2] and special cardiology. It was suggested that the most closely related and co-operating departments should join in blocs, e.g. the Neuro-Psychiatry bloc, the Thoracic bloc. Further on, 'jaw units' (surgery, orthodontics, prosthetics) and units for renal diseases including artificial kidney treatment were recommended.

The following laboratory services were proposed: paediatric X-ray departments, virological, allergological and blood-coagulation laboratories, laboratories for hormone analysis, for cytology and for isotope diagnostics and therapy ('hot laboratories').

As can be realized from the study of Table 14, specialization

[1] Godlund: Population, regional hospitals, transport facilities, and regions. Royal University of Lund, Sweden, 1961.
[2] Against my recommendation.

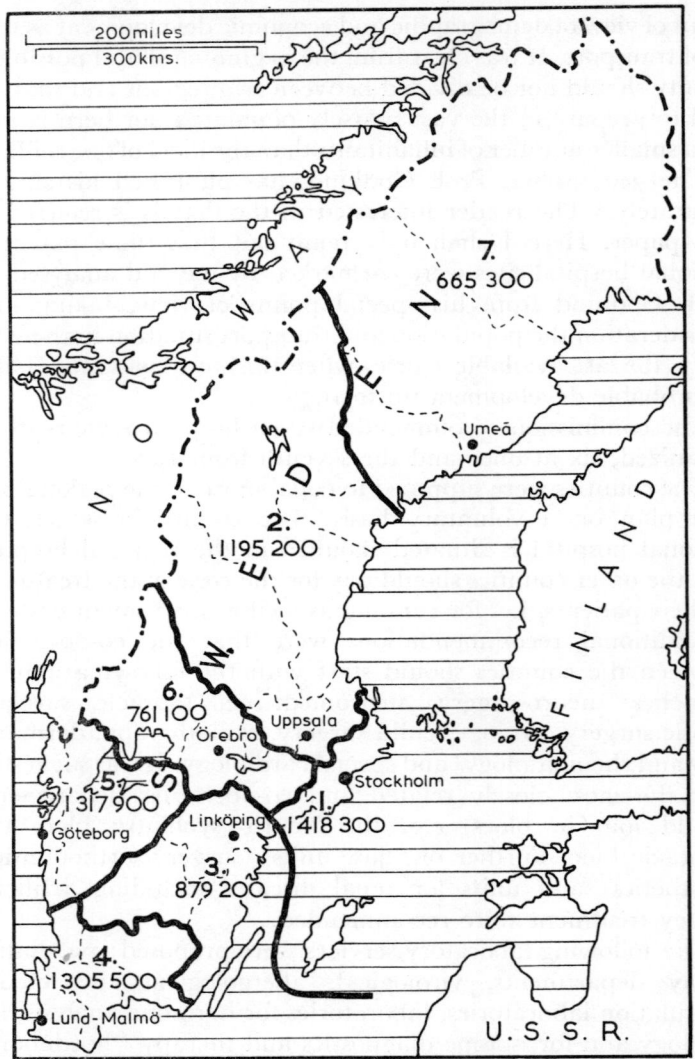

Fig. 19. The seven hospital regions with site of the regional hospital and number of inhabitants. Dotted lines mark the borders of the counties.

in the surgical field has been largely embarked upon whereas great concern has been taken not to break up internal medicine too much. I always felt that specialization in medicine should mainly be based on technological grounds. This attitude seems to me to guarantee the integration of medical care of the individual in the best possible way. I therefore suggested that cardiology should in principle be kept under the department of internal medicine, but that a small technical unit of about 30 beds should be arranged for advanced diagnostic procedures (catheterization on the arterial side, etc.). This unit should co-operate closely with thoracic surgery, chest clinic, clinical physiology and radiology, i.e. that it should be a part of the thoracic bloc. Endocrinology with its very close connections with metabolism will remain inside internal medicine and the technical provisions will be offered by a special agency, the hormone laboratory.

From the emerging young specialist there is a strong demand for separate departments for each specialty while the old clinicians are in favour of having them ass ubdivisions of departments of medicine and general surgery. My own attitude and my recommendations were, for reasons already mentioned, in favour of the independence of branches of surgery and subordination of most of the new offspring of internal medicine under the mother discipline.

The plan was with slight modifications presented by the cabinet to Parliament in 1960. The main change, made in the cabinet Bill, was that the seven regions should be established right from the start. Parliament accepted the plan.

### AFTERMATH OF THE REGIONAL HOSPITAL PLAN

The application of the regional hospital plan in practice has gone very smoothly up to date. The counties of each region have set up a joint standing agency for co-ordination (the regional health care committee) advising the county councils with which the final decision lies.

Through this Act of Parliament, Sweden obtained a regionalized hospital system with regional hospitals, county central hospitals and peripheral hospitals called normal or district hospitals. The map (on page 78) illustrates the geography, the number of inhabitants of the regions and the site of the regional hospitals at present. In the early seventies Stockholm (already more or less a double region) will have two full teaching hospitals and the number of regions will become eight.

The philosophy of the regionalized hospital system was received by health authorities and the medical profession in the most favourable way.

The prediction that *every regional hospital* should be regarded as *a potential teaching hospital* has proved to be true. Since the plan was presented in 1958 a university with a medical faculty has been founded at Umeå and decided upon at Linköping while a seventh is expected to be built at Örebro.

*The regional hospital* has proved to be *a most important centre of clinical research.* The medical faculty of Umeå has been extraordinarily instrumental in providing the sparsely populated northern hospital region with scientifically trained clinicians.

*The regional hospital* has served as *a core for the development* of new specialized services. I will mention these referring to Table 15 which shows the new departments and other services incorporated or attached to the regional hospitals whether established or only decided upon.

One amendment to the original plan was made in 1963. It was found inadvisable to carry out advanced cardiac surgery needing extracorporeal circulation and respiration by means of the heart-lung machine at all regional hospitals. This activity is therefore now located in the four largest regions only. Further, no new departments of rheumatology have been organized at the regional level. I do not regret this as I still hold the opinion that the rheumatics should be taken care of at the county level.

There seems to be complete agreement on the observation that the creation of the regional level has prevented duplication of services and irrational use of personnel and resources. Wrong investments have thus been avoided. The regions suggested by me serve an average of roughly 1 million inhabitants. Where the number is a little smaller, as in the sparsely populated northern part of the country, the evolution seems to be lagging behind. On the other hand there has been no disadvantage with $1\frac{1}{2}$

TABLE 15. New regional services since 1961.

| In-services | Attached services | Independent regional institutions |
|---|---|---|
| Department of Rheumatology<br>Department of Occupational Medicine<br>Kidney Units, composed of<br>  Department of Nephrology<br>  Department of Urology<br>  Centre for Haemodialysis<br>Department of Child Neurology<br>Clinical Neuro Physiology<br>Neurological Rehabilitation<br>Department of Clinical Pharmacology<br>Phoniatric Clinics<br>Audiological Laboratory | Department of Social Medicine<br>Homes for Mentally Disturbed Children (operated from the Department of Child Psychiatry)<br>Unit for Children with Cerebral Palsy and allied CNS disorders (attached to the Department of Child Neurology or Paediatrics) | Mental Retardation (multiple disability, low-grades) |

million, rather, I would say, an advantage, in that development has been more rapid there.

The regional hospital plan has, of course, been further elaborated at all levels and has resulted in a regionalized health system. The idea that a region should be an area that is independent and self-supporting in health services has been generally accepted and *the region* (the inter-county level) has been found *an appropriate level at which to undertake planning of health services*. The most outstanding medical experts are available here. A group of politicians and administrators from the participating counties constitute the co-ordinating body of the region. They are competent to present statements on the socio-economic development of different parts of the region; they know the demand and needs of the population and can give a true picture of the present, and they should be consulted as to how to assess the trends of the future. They have to weigh the demands of the technical experts and pick out what they deem to be realistic from the financial point of view.

The repercussions of the regionalized approach as regards the health services can best be understood from Fig. 9 on page 19.

This figure shows the levels of organization of hospital care (regional, county and local). The public, extramural medical care provided by district doctors (provinsialläkare) is added by presenting the health centres at the base of the pyramid.

At the level next to the *regional hospital* we find the *central hospital of the county*. These institutions are more and more becoming the leading centres for all medical and socio-medical activities inside the counties. They comprise as a rule 800–1000 beds, large out-patient departments (typical for Swedish hospitals!), rehabilitation centre, mother and child welfare services, family planning and advisory centres, nursing school, dental services, etc.

Among the different specialties should be observed departments for psychiatry and for child psychiatry. Much importance is placed on close integration of somatic and psychiatric care.

The next organizational county level is the 'normal hospital' —the *local district hospital*. These hospitals have for many years been a headache to the national health administration. Many of them have been too small, serving too small a population, or have been wrongly located. They do not meet the requirements of modern surgery and therefore cannot give emergency service around the clock, and so on. They have been difficult to staff, especially as regards doctors. Our policy—carried on against remarkable resistance from local authorities and the local press—urgently stressed that all hospitals should have specialized departments for surgery, medicine, anaesthesiology, X-ray, obstetrics and gynaecology, paediatrics, psychiatry, and long-term diseases (mainly geriatrics), with a total of about 300 beds. The population in the area to be covered should be at least 60 000 and preferably 90 000 inhabitants. The other district hospitals should be converted into nursing homes for long-term diseases, or health centres, or—even better—a combination of both, which has been found to be very rational.

The lowest organizational level for public medical care—the local commune (township) is represented by the *health centre* providing a population of 10 000–20 000 with ambulatory preventive and curative care. To the health centre is attached a *peripheral home for long-term illness* (cf. Fig. 10). These centres, still under development, are not part of the hospital organization, but our aim is to integrate their activities as closely as possible with the nearest district hospital. A goal as yet nowhere achieved is to have an exchange of medical personnel, primarily doctors, between the hospital and the health centres. May I add also that we nourish the hope of having our health centres staffed, in the future, with specialists in internal medicine, paediatrics, obstetrics and gynaecology, psychiatry, with a doctor of social medicine as a co-ordinator and leader. This would mean a more effective pattern of medical practice.

I would like to mention private practice in parenthesis. We encourage the establishment of group practice, preferably by specialists. Personally I feel that it is true already and will be more so in the future that no doctor can cover the whole rapidly expanding field of medicine as a diagnostician and therapist of all kinds of illnesses. This includes even the so-called minor diseases, or rather what are thought of as minor diseases.

*For the large cities,* Greater-Stockholm (1 300 000), Gothenburg

(500 000), and Malmö (250 000), *the application of the regionalized hospital system had to be modified.* In principle this means that there is no longer a marked distinction between central hospitals and district hospitals. The hospital plan for the city and county of Stockholm is presented in the Fig. 20 as a good example of regionalization inside a metropolitan area. *The annex hospital is an interesting new type of institution constructed for the care of chronic illnesses and with excellent rehabilitation facilities and an outpatient department.* The patients are admitted from the central and district hospitals of the sector to which the annex hospital belongs, as indicated on the diagram.

The main goal of the regionalized hospital system is to

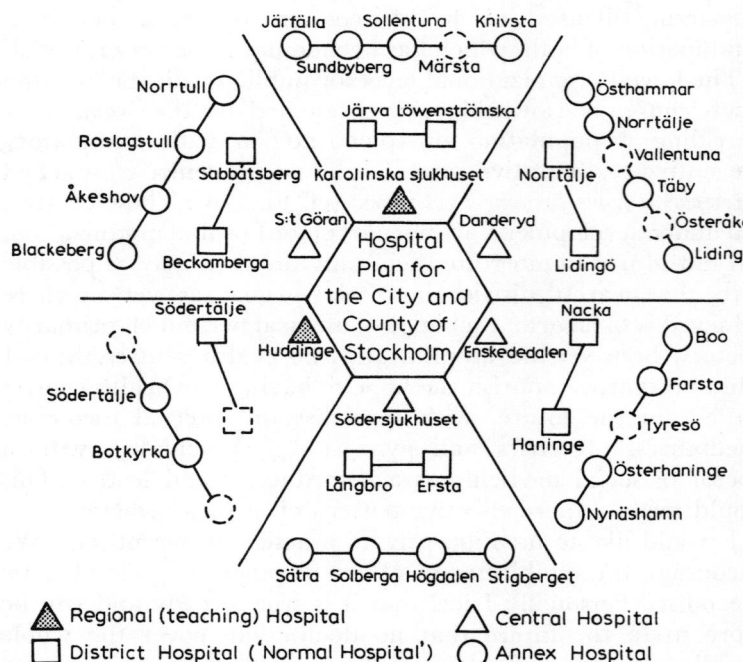

FIG. 20. Hospital Plan for Greater Stockholm. Dotted lines indicate hospitals to be built after 1975.

provide qualified medical treatment for the population in every area of the country. This can only be achieved when qualified specialists are available, heading special departments, big enough to be well staffed and equipped so that they can be the site of specialist-training and of clinical research (roughly 40–60 beds).

If we had not launched the regional hospital system we would have witnessed the growth of small specialist services in many places—a duplication of services. They would not have had the capacity to develop the highest quality of care and to keep abreast of scientific progress. That would have meant a bad investment of funds and of medical personnel. The regionalized system, on the contrary, makes the feasible optimum use of investment and personnel. At the same time it makes high-quality specialist care available to everybody in the country.

At all organizational levels we demand high quality of care and are trying to ensure that the services keep up to this. On the other hand, as I said earlier, we have to think of the convenience of the public and are therefore anxious not to centralize too much particularly in remote and sparsely populated areas. Therefore, and for financial and manpower reasons, we have formulated the guiding principle that *care should be provided at the lowest acceptable organizational level of the health system.*

Thus the old balance between centralization and decentralization of hospital services is still there. However, modern medicine and technology favour centralization, and so does the development of modern society itself. We should be aware of this.

## REFERENCES

S.O.U. (*Swedish Government Official Reports*) 1958, **26**. The Regional Hospital Plan. Stockholm: Socialdepartementet (Ministry for Social Affairs).

S.O.U. (*Swedish Government Official Reports*) 1961, **8**. Future supply and need of Doctors. Stockholm: Socialdepartementet (Ministry for Social Affairs).

MARSTON, R. and VORDY, K. (1967) A Nation starts a program: Regional Medical Programs 1965–66 *J. M. Educ.* **42**.

MARSTON, R. (1967) Regional medical programs the next steps. Presentation at the American Hospital Association annual meeting. Not yet published.

TOTTIE and JANZON (ed.) (1967) *Regional Hospital Planning.* Valedictory volume dedicated to Arthur Engel. Stockholm: Nordiska Bokhandeln. The following articles of this book have been taken in to consideration:

LINDGREN, S. Yesterday-today-tomorrow. A close up of the regional hospital plan. Ibid. 45.
CANDAU, M. G. Health planning in the regional context. Ibid. 53.
CROSBY (ed.) The international hospital Federation and the planning of medical care. Ibid. 90.
GOOSSENS, J. F. La programmation hospitalière en Belgique. Ibid. 100.
AUJALEU, E. La planification hospitalière en France. Ibid. 120.
GODBER, Sir George, Health planning in Great Britain. Ibid. 131.
U.S. DEPARTMENT OF HEALTH, EDUCATION AND WELFARE. PUBLIC HEALTH SERVICE. (1967) *Regional Medical Programs*, Bethesda, Md, Division of Regional Medical Programs. National Institutes of Health.
LLEWELYN-DAVIES, R. and MACAULAY, H. M. C. (1966) *Hospital Planning and Administration.* Geneva: WHO.
MC KEOWN, T. (1965) A *Balanced Teaching Hospital.* Published for the Nuffield Provincial Hospitals Trust. London: Oxford University Press.

# INDEX

Accidents, 6–7
Ambulatory and domiciliary care, 23
Asymptomatic disease, 47–8
Automation, 3

Bed/population rates (bed quotas), 71–3, 76; for superspecialties, 75–6
Bed situation summer 1965, 39

Care, of the aged, 21–3; lowest acceptable level of, 85
Causes of death, 12, 30
Changing society, 1; affluence, 4; age distribution, 10; epoch of education, 5; establishment, opposition against, 3; family life, 3; industrialization, 3; nuclear energy, 9; science, 2; service rendering, 4; synthetic environment, 9, 21; technology, 2; urbanization, 3
Child psychiatry, 5, 20–1
Clinical genetics, 18
Commission on Hospital Planning and Equipment, 72
Community self-government, 70
Consumer unit, 10, 72
County, 19–20, 71
County council, 70, 74

Danish Morbidity Study, 12, 31
Demographic and vital statistics, 27
Disability pension, 37; distribution by disease group, 15–17; role of mental retardation and CNS-damage, 37
Disease and disability, pattern of, 11–16
Drug consumption, 8
Duration of disease, the 90-day investigation, 14–15

Ephebiatrics, 6
Expectation of life, 27

Food additives, 7

Gregg, N. M., 29
Gross national product, 23

Health care usage, 10–11
Health centres, 20, 83
Health insurance statistics, 13–17, 37
Health policy for the modern society, 17; integrated medical and social service, 18
Hospital morbidity statistics, 34–5
Hospital, requirement for beds, 71; catchment area of, 19–20, 71, 76, 80, 83; central, 20, 71, 82; district (normal), 20, 72, 74, 82–3; regional, 19, 76–82; size of, 19, 82–3; system, 18
Human ecology and ethology, 5–6

Identity number (civil registration number), 35
Immunology, 18
Infant mortality, 27–9
Investments, 22–3

Jungner laboratory, 50–1

Kaiser Permanente Organization, 49

Labour-force, 3, 23
Lenz, W., 29
Local commune, 20
Loneliness, 6
Long-term illness, 22–3, 84

Maternity mortality, 27

Medical alert statistics, 42; abortions, 42; adverse effects of drugs, 42; cancer register, 42; malformation register, 42; stillbirth, 42
Medical life-time records bank, 36
Mental retardation, 15, 20
Morbidity and disability statistics, 30; the 15th born sample, 33; health insurance statistics, 30–1; sample of population, 31; continuous population sample, 31; rotated sample, 33; United States National Health Survey, 33

National Board of Health, 18
National Board of Health and Welfare, 18
Nursing homes, 22

Pediatrics, modern trends, 20
Photofluorography, general mass, 49–50
Poisoning, 6–7
Poison information centre, 8
Population, distribution by age, 27–8; migration, 27
Prenatal and perinatal research, 29
Preventive measures, 23
Priority standards, 55 and appendix 1
Psychiatric disease, 15
Psychiatry, 5, 20–1

Regional hospital plan, 72, 74–9; modified for large cities, 83–4
Regionalized health system, 82
Register of medical and paramedical personnel, 39
Rehabilitation centre, 82
Running cost, 23

Sensory deprivation, 6
Socio-economic development, 1
Statistics, facilities and resources, 39; health personnel, 39, 41–2; health services activity, 38
Stillbirth, 29
Stresses and strains of modern life, 6
Superspecialties, 75–9

Teaching hospital, 80
Toxicology, 6–9, 18
Training programmes, 21
Twin register, 44

UN Development Decade, 1

Värmland trial, 50; costs, 62; evaluation, 60–2; field area, 52–3; follow-up results, 57; population, 53–4; procedure, 54–6; programme, 54

Youth, as consumer group, 5; and family, 3; as pressure group, 5